Lets Learn

ASP — Advanced Server Pages

Abhishek Dayal

P Mithunish

Dear Readers,

In order to make beautiful and dynamic web pages ASP provides students must develop both a foundation of communication skills and an under- standing of the key elements critical to achieving group success.

Abhishek Dayal
P Mithunish

ASP- Microsoft Active Server Pages

Developed by Microsoft in 16-July-1996 as a powerful & easy technology to create dynamic web pages. Simple to use & extensible. You can combine HTML pages, scripts & activex components to create interactive web pages. Allows you to generate the browser-neutral contents using server side scripting.

The key component of ASP is a dedicated web server. ASP provides better communication between browser & server with release of Internet Information Server (IIS 4.0) & Personal Web Server (PWS).

ASP page is any file located on web server that has extension .asp. When ASP page has been requested, before sending a page to users browser, it is processed by web server. It interprets and executes any scripts in ASP page before sending it to users browser.

Understanding client-server model

Client – Requests the resources.
Server – Provides the resources.

Types of web pages – static & dynamic.
When web browser requests an ASP, it follows steps-
1. the client/web browser locates the web server specified by first part of URL.
2. Client requests a ASP page.
3. Server reads the ASP file & process code.
4. Server returns HTML format to client.

ASP vs Client Side Scripting

The 2 types of scripting are –
1. Client side – the over use of client side scripting can result in large files that take a long time to download. Runs or executed on browser. Reduces work of server & network traffic. Is commonly written using JavaScript because Netscape Navigator only supports this for client-side scripting.
2. Server Side- Requires because the need for active web sites. The benefits are –
   a. Protects the code
   b. Enables web application to access database.
   c. The page contents can be retrieved from database, text files & other data sources. Then can be inserted using HTML code dynamically before displayed to users.
   d. Allows to develop web application such that change in HTML design doesn't affect the programs that retrieve data from database. Changing data sources will not require to change HTML document.
   e. Use this when access to data that resides anywhere except client.

Setting PWS or IIS

1. PWS – Personal Web Server, works with Windows 95,98 or NT workstation. Prototypes a web site before you transfer contents to IIS. It is a scale down version of web server.

How to install PWS and run ASP on Windows 98

1. Open the **Add-ons** folder on your Windows98 CD, find the **PWS** folder and run the **setup.exe** file.
2. An **Inetpub folder** will be created on your harddrive. Open it and find the **wwwroot** folder.
3. **Create a new folder**, like "MyWeb", under wwwroot.
4. **Use a text editor** to write some ASP code, save the file as "test1.asp" in the "MyWeb" folder.
5. Make sure your Web server is running - The installation program has added a new icon on your task bar (this is the PWS symbol). Click on the icon and press the Start button in the window that appears.
6. **Open your browser** and type in "http://localhost/MyWeb/test1.asp", to view your first ASP page.

PWS contains 5 sections –

1. Main – Contains statistical information about site. Ex. Requests per hour, req. per day etc.
2. Advanced – User can alter permissions through this. Contains web site directory structure.
3. Publish
4. Website
5. Tour

Used to host a very low traffic web site.

2. IIS – Internet Information Server

IIS is a professional web server. Usually provided with Windows 2000(IIS 5.0) for Windows NT (IIS 4.0)

Can be downloaded from
http://www.microsoft.com/msdownload/ntoptionpack/askwiz.asp

To launch IIS manager choose start – programs – admin tools.

Internet Service Manager of IIS allows you to configure your web site, FTP Server & SMTP service. MS Management Console (MMC) used to configure IIS & other admin tasks.

Creating ASP pages using tools – To create an ASP page you can use notepad or ASP tools like
1. Visual Interdev – is a development environment for building web sites. Fancy text editor to create, modify web pages on remote or local server. You can use it fore both writing ASP pages and HTML pages. It makes easier to manage pages of large web sites. Also includes debugging tools. You can allow drag & drop option for objects.
2. Front Page – is a Microsoft tool that you can use to develop individual web site or pages. Provided various views for many options like Page, Folders, Navigations, Hyperlinks, and Tasks. User can switch between

normal, HTML or Preview tabs. In front page the web refers to a domain name or subdirectories where you will place a web site.

To differentiate where ASP code starts & ends <%   %> tags are used.

1. Request object

Collections

a. Form -

The Form collection is used to retrieve the values of form elements from a form that uses the POST method.

If you want to post large amounts of data (beyond 100 kb) the Request.Form cannot be used.

Syntax - Request.Form (element)[(index)|. Count]

Parameter	Description
element	Required. The name of the form element from which the collection is to retrieve values
index	Optional. Specifies one of multiple values for a parameter. From 1 to Request.Form (parameter). Count.

Examples

Example 1

You can loop through all the values in a form request. If a user filled out a form by specifying two values - Blue and Green - for the color element, you could retrieve those values like this:

```
<%
for i=1 to Request.Form("color").Count
        Response.Write(Request.Form("color")(i) & "<br />")
Next %>
```

Output:

Blue
Green

b. QueryString

The QueryString collection is used to retrieve the variable values in the HTTP query string.

The HTTP query string is specified by the values following the question mark (?), like this:

<a href= "test.asp?txt=this is a query string test">Link with a query string</a>

The line above generates a variable named txt with the value "this is a query string test".

Query strings are also generated by form submission, or by a user typing a query into the address bar of the browser.

Syntax - Request.QueryString(variable)[(index)|.Count]

Parameter	Description
variable	Required. The name of the variable in the HTTP query string to retrieve
Index	Optional. Specifies one of multiple values for a variable. From 1 to Request.QuerString(variable).Count

c. ServerVariables

The ServerVariables collection is used to retrieve the server variable values.

Syntax - Request.ServerVariables (server_variable)

Parameter	Description
server_variable	Required. The name of the server variable to retrieve

Server Variables

Variable	Description
ALL_HTTP	Returns all HTTP headers sent by the client. Always prefixed with HTTP_ and capitalized
ALL_RAW	Returns all headers in raw form
APPL_PHYSICAL_PATH	Returns the physical path corresponding to the meta base path
AUTH_PASSWORD	Returns the value entered in the client's authentication dialog
AUTH_TYPE	The authentication method that the server uses to validate users
AUTH_USER	Returns the raw authenticated user name
CERT_COOKIE	Returns the unique ID for client certificate as a string
CERT_FLAGS	bit0 is set to 1 if the client certificate is present and bit1 is set to 1 if the certification authority of the client certificate is not valid
CERT_ISSUER	Returns the issuer field of the client certificate

CERT_KEYSIZE	Returns the number of bits in Secure Sockets Layer connection key size
CERT_SECRETKEYSIZE	Returns the number of bits in server certificate private key
CERT_SERIALNUMBER	Returns the serial number field of the client certificate
CERT_SERVER_ISSUER	Returns the issuer field of the server certificate
CERT_SERVER_SUBJECT	Returns the subject field of the server certificate
CERT_SUBJECT	Returns the subject field of the client certificate
CONTENT_LENGTH	Returns the length of the content as sent by the client
CONTENT_TYPE	Returns the data type of the content
GATEWAY_INTERFACE	Returns the revision of the CGI specification used by the server
HTTP_<*HeaderName*>	Returns the value stored in the header *HeaderName*
HTTP_ACCEPT	Returns the value of the Accept header
HTTP_ACCEPT_LANGUAGE	Returns a string describing the language to use for displaying content
HTTP_COOKIE	Returns the cookie string included with the request
HTTP_REFERER	Returns a string containing the URL of the page that referred the request to the current page using an <a> tag. If the page is redirected, HTTP_REFERER is empty
HTTP_USER_AGENT	Returns a string describing the browser that sent the request
HTTPS	Returns ON if the request came in through secure channel or OFF if the request came in through a non-secure channel
HTTPS_KEYSIZE	Returns the number of bits in Secure Sockets Layer connection key size
HTTPS_SECRETKEYSIZE	Returns the number of bits in server certificate private key
HTTPS_SERVER_ISSUER	Returns the issuer field of the server certificate
HTTPS_SERVER_SUBJECT	Returns the subject field of the server certificate
INSTANCE_ID	The ID for the IIS instance in text format
INSTANCE_META_PATH	The meta base path for the instance of IIS that responds to the request
LOCAL_ADDR	Returns the server address on which the request came in
LOGON_USER	Returns the Windows account that the user is logged into
PATH_INFO	Returns extra path information as given by the client
PATH_TRANSLATED	A translated version of PATH_INFO that takes the path and performs any necessary virtual-to-physical mapping

QUERY_STRING	Returns the query information stored in the string following the question mark (?) in the HTTP request
REMOTE_ADDR	Returns the IP address of the remote host making the request
REMOTE_HOST	Returns the name of the host making the request
REMOTE_USER	Returns an unmapped user-name string sent in by the user
REQUEST_METHOD	Returns the method used to make the request
SCRIPT_NAME	Returns a virtual path to the script being executed
SERVER_NAME	Returns the server's host name, DNS alias, or IP address as it would appear in self-referencing URLs
SERVER_PORT	Returns the port number to which the request was sent
SERVER_PORT_SECURE	Returns a string that contains 0 or 1. If the request is being handled on the secure port, it will be 1. Otherwise, it will be 0
SERVER_PROTOCOL	Returns the name and revision of the request information protocol
SERVER_SOFTWARE	Returns the name and version of the server software that answers the request and runs the gateway
URL	Returns the base portion of the URL

Example 1

You can loop through all of the server variables like this:

```
<%
for each x in Request.ServerVariables
  response.write(x & "<br />")
next
%>
```

Example 2

This example demonstrates how to find out the visitor's browser type, IP address, and more:

```
<html>
<body>
<p> <b>You are browsing this site with:</b>
<%Response.Write(Request.ServerVariables("http_user_agent"))%>
</p>
<p><b>Your IP address is:</b>
<%Response.Write(Request.ServerVariables("remote_addr"))%>
</p>
```

```
<p><b>The DNS lookup of the IP address is:</b>
<%Response.Write(Request.ServerVariables("remote_host"))%>
</p>
<p><b>The method used to call the page:</b>
<%Response.Write(Request.ServerVariables("request_method"))%>
</p>
<p><b>The server's domain name:</b>
<%Response.Write(Request.ServerVariables("server_name"))%>
</p>
<p><b>The server's port:</b>
<%Response.Write(Request.ServerVariables("server_port"))%>
</p>
<p><b>The server's software:</b>
<%Response.Write(Request.ServerVariables("server_software"))%>
</p> </body></html>
```

d. Cookies –
- Uses to store information on a customers computer when customer visit your web site. You can use this information to identify customer once again, whenever customer returns to your site.
- You can store visitors username, preferences like favorite product, place etc.

Two types of cookies are-
1. Session - stored in memory & remains on customers computer only while customer is visiting your web site.
2. Persistent- can last many months or years. Stored in text file on customers computer called Cookie file.
In Netscape all persistent cookies from all web sites will get stores in "cookies.txt" file under /Netscape or /Netscape/user/username folder. Ms-Internet Explorer creates a separate cookie file for each web site located in /windows/cookies folder. A web site can read only the cookies it has set.

Cookies are not reliable because –
1. Privacy worries- User can disabled cookies from browser
2. Cookies files can be deleted or corrupted.
3. Visitor may access website from a machine that is different from where the cookies was placed.

Limitations of Cookies-
1. A single computer can hold maximum 300 cookies from all web sites.
2. Single website cann't add more than 20 cookies to customers computer.
3. An individual cookie cannot hold data more than 4kb.

A cookie can be simple or complex.
-Simple cookie contains a single value.
        Ex- value=Request.Cookies(""username")
-Complex – contains more than one value within a single cookie.
        Ex- un=Request.Cookies("user")("username")
                upass=Request.Cookies("user")("userpass")

- To check whether   the cookie is simple or complex use HasKeys which returns true or false.

      If Request.cookies("user").HasKeys then
          Response.write "complex"
      Else
          Response.write "Simple"
      End if

e. ClientCertificate

      - To identify visitors use ClientCertificates.
      - Users can purchase a client certificate from an organization called Certificate Authority (CA), which is a company that creates certificates for individual.
      - You can retrieve objects like-ValidUntil, ISSUER
ex- To see all values in certificate

```
<% for each cvalue in Request.ClientCertificate
     Response.write cvalue & ":" & Request.ClientCertificate (cvalue) & "<p>"
   next
%>
```

Property

The **TotalBytes** property is a read-only property that returns the total number of bytes the client sent in the body of the request.

Syntax - varbytes=Request.Totalbytes

Example

The following code sets the variable a equal to the total number of bytes sent in the body of the request:

```
<%
dim a
a=Request.TotalBytes
response.write "total bytes-" & a
%>
```

Method

The **BinaryRead** method is used to retrieve the data sent to the server from the client as part of a POST request. It will store the data in a safe array (an array that stores information about the number of dimensions and the bounds of its dimensions).

Note: A call to Request.Form after a call to BinaryRead, and vice-versa, will cause an error.

Syntax - Request.BinaryRead(count)

Parameter	Description
count	Required. Specifies how many bytes to read from the client

Examples

The following example uses the BinaryRead method to place the content of a request into a safe array:

```
<%
dim a,b
a=Request.TotalBytes
b=Request.BinaryRead(a)
%>
```

2. Response Object

The ASP Response object is used to send output to the user from the server. Its collections, properties, and methods are described below:

Collections

The Cookies collection is used to set or get cookie values. If the cookie does not exist, it will be created, and take the value that is specified.

Note: The Response.Cookies command must appear before the <html> tag.

Syntax

Response.Cookies(name)[(key)|.attribute]=value
variablename=Request.Cookies(name)[(key)|.attribute]

Parameter	Description
name	Required. The name of the cookie
value	Required for the Response.Cookies command. The value of the cookie
attribute	Optional. Specifies information about the cookie. Can be one of the following parameters:

- Domain - Write-only. The cookie is sent only to requests to this domain
- Expires - Write-only. The date when the cookie expires. If no date is specified, the cookie will expire when the session ends

- HasKeys - Read-only. Specifies whether the cookie has keys (This is the only attribute that can be used with the Request. Cookies command)
- Path - Write-only. If set, the cookie is sent only to requests to this path. If not set, the application path is used
- Secure - Write-only. Indicates if the cookie is secure key Optional. Specifies the key to where the value is assigned

Examples

The "Response.Cookies" command is used to create a cookie or to set a cookie value:

```
<%  Response.Cookies("firstname")="Alex" %>
```

In the code above, we have created a cookie named "firstname" and assigned the value "Alex" to it.

It is also possible to assign some attributes to a cookie, like setting a date when a cookie should expire:

```
<%
Response.Cookies("firstname")="Alex"
Response.Cookies("firstname").Expires=#May 10,2002#
%>
```

Now the cookie named "firstname" has the value of "Alex", and it will expire from the user's computer at May 10, 2002.

The "Request.Cookies" command is used to get a cookie value.

In the example below, we retrieve the value of the cookie "firstname" and display it on a page:
```
<% fname=Request.Cookies("firstname")
response.write("Firstname=" & fname)
%>
```
Output:

Firstname=Alex

A cookie can also contain a collection of multiple values. We say that the cookie has Keys.

In the example below, we will create a cookie-collection named "user". The "user" cookie has Keys that contains information about a user:

```
<%
Response.Cookies("user")("firstname")="John"
Response.Cookies("user")("lastname")="Smith"
Response.Cookies("user")("country")="Norway"
```

```
Response.Cookies("user")("age")="25"
%>
```

The code below reads all the cookies your server has sent to a user. Note that the code checks if a cookie has Keys with the HasKeys property:

```
<html> <body>
<%
dim x,y
for each x in Request.Cookies
  response.write("<p>")
  if Request.Cookies(x).HasKeys then
    for each y in Request.Cookies(x)
      response.write(x & ":" & y & "=" & Request.Cookies(x)(y))
      response.write("<br />")
    next
  else
    Response.Write(x & "=" & Request.Cookies(x) & "<br />")
  end if
  response.write "</p>"
next
%> </body> </html> %>
```

Output:

firstname=Alex

user:firstname=John
user:lastname=Smith
user: country=Norway
user: age=25

Format in which text stored in Cookie is
        - First line shows cookie name, second shows value stored to their hexadecimal equivalent. Some other characters like New line char. will be displayed as black box, / by %2F, space by +, colon by %3A etc.

Advantages of Cookies
1. Can store small amount of information for long periods.
2. As cookies are stored on client, no need to locate space on web site to store user specific information.
3. Used to customize a users visit to web site.

Properties

a. Buffer -

The Buffer property specifies whether to buffer the output or not. When the output is buffered, the server will hold back the response to the browser until all of the server scripts have been processed, or until the script calls the Flush or End method.

Note: If this property is set, it should be before the <html> tag in the .asp file

Syntax

Response.Buffer[=flag]

Parameter	Description
flag	A boolean value that specifies whether to buffer the page output or not.

False indicates no buffering. The server will send the output as it is processed. False is default for IIS version 4.0 (and earlier). Default for IIS version 5.0 (and later) is true.

True indicates buffering. The server will not send output until all of the   scripts on the page have been processed, or until the Flush or End method has   been called.

Examples

Example 1

In this example, there will be no output sent to the browser before the loop is finished. If buffer was set to False, then it would write a line to the browser every time it went through the loop.

```
<%response. Buffer=true%>
<html> <body>
<%
for i=1 to 100
        response.write(i & "<br />")
next
%>
</body> </html>
```

Example 2

```
<%response.Buffer=true%>
        <html> <body>
                <p>I write some text, but I will control when
                the text will be sent to the browser.</p>
                <p>The text is not sent yet. I hold it back!</p>
                <p>OK, let it go!</p>
<%response.Flush%>
</body> </html>
```

Example 3

```
<%response.Buffer=true%>
<html> <body>
        <p>This is some text I want to send to the user.</p>
```

```
    <p>No, I changed my mind. I want to clear the text.</p>
<%response.Clear%>
</body> </html>
```

b. CacheControl

The CacheControl property sets whether a proxy server can cache the output generated by ASP or not. By default, a proxy server will not keep a cache copy.

Syntax

response.CacheControl[=control_header]

Parameter	Description
control_header	A cache control header that can be set to "Public" or "Private".

Private is default and indicates that only private caches may cache this page. Proxy servers will not cache pages with this setting.

Public indicates public caches. Proxy servers will cache pages with this setting.

Examples

<%response.CacheControl="Public"%>

or

<%response.CacheControl="Private"%>

c. CharSet –
Allows you to modify CharSet parameter of content type header.
Response.CharSet = "characterValue"
Value represents name of character set you wish to use.

The Charset property appends the name of a character-set to the content-type header in the Response object. Default character set is ISO-LATIN-1.

Note: This property will accept any string, regardless of whether it is a valid character set or not, for the name.

Syntax

Response. Charset (charsetname)

Parameter	Description
charsetname	A string that specifies a character set for the page

Examples
If an ASP page has no Charset property set, the content-type header would be:
Content-type:text/html
If we included the Charset property:
    <%Response. Charset="ISO-8859-1"%>
The content-type header would be:
        Content-type: text/html; charset=ISO-8859-1

d. ContentType –
The ContentType property sets the HTTP content type for the response object.

Syntax
response.ContentType[=contenttype]

Parameter	Description
contenttype	A string describing the content type.

Examples
If an ASP page has no ContentType property set, the default content-type header would be:
content-type:text/html. Some other common ContentType values:
        <%response.ContentType="text/HTML"%>
        <%response.ContentType="image/GIF"%>
        <%response.ContentType="image/JPEG"%>
        <%response.ContentType="text/plain"%>
        <%response.ContentType="image/JPEG"%>

This example will open an Excel spreadsheet in a browser (if the user has Excel installed):

```
<%response.ContentType="application/vnd.ms-excel"%>
<html> <body> <table>
<tr>     <td>1</td>
        <td>2</td>
        <td>3</td>
        <td>4</td>
</tr>
<tr>     <td>5</td>
        <td>6</td>
        <td>7</td>
        <td>8</td>
</tr>
</table> </body> </html>
```

e. Expires-

The Expires property sets how long (in minutes) a page will be cached on a browser before it expires. If a user returns to the same page before it expires, the cached version is displayed.

Syntax
Response.Expires[=number]

Parameter	Description
number	The time in minutes before the page expires

Examples

Example 1

The following code indicates that the page will never be cached:

<%response.Expires=-1%>

Example 2

The following code indicates that the page will expire after 1440 minutes (24 hours):

<%response.Expires=1440%>

f. ExpiresAbsolute
The ExpiresAbsolute property sets a date and time when a cached page on a browser will expire. If a user returns to the same page before this date/time, the cached version is displayed.

Syntax
Response. ExpiresAbsolute[=[date][time]]

Parameter	Description
Date	Specifies the date on which the page will expire. If this parameter is not specified, the page will expire at the specified time on the day that the script is run.
Time	Specifies the time at which the page will expire. If this parameter is not specified, the page will expire at midnight of the specified day.

Examples

The following code indicates that the page will expire at 4:00 PM on October 11, 2003:
<%response.ExpiresAbsolute=#October 11,2003 16:00:00#%>

g. IsClientConnected

The IsClientConnected property indicates if the client has disconnected from the server.

Syntax

response.IsClientConnected

Examples

```
<%
If response.IsClientConnected=true then
      response.write("The user is still connected!")
else
      response.write("The user is not connected!")
end if
%>
```

h. PICS

The PICS property appends a value to the PICS label response header. **Note:** This property will accept any string value, regardless of whether it is a valid PICS label or not.

The PICS (Platform for Internet Content Selection) rating system is used to rate the content in a web site. It looks something like this:

PICS-1.1 "http://www.rsac.org/ratingsv01.html" by "your@name.com" for "http://www.somesite.com" on "2002.10.05T02:15-0800" r (n 0 s 0 v 0 l 0)

Part	Description
PICS-1.1	PICS version number
"http://www.rsac.org/ratingsv01.html"	Rating organization
by "your@name.com"	Author of the label
for "http://www.somesite.com"	The URL or the document that has been rated
on "2002.10.05T02:15-0800"	Expiration date
r (n 0 s 0 v 0 l 0)	Rating

One of the most popular rating system is RSACi (Recreational Software Advisory Council on the Internet). RSACi rating system uses four categories: violence, nudity, sex, and language. A number between 0 to 4 is assigned to each category. 0 means that the page does not contain any potentially offensive content and 4 means that the page contains the highest levels of potentially offensive content.

There are two ways you can obtain rating for your site. You can either rate your side yourself or use a rating provider, like RSACi. They'll ask you fill out some questions. After filling out the questions, you will get the rating label for your site. Microsoft IE 3.0 and above and Netscape 4.5 and above support the content ratings. You can set the ratings in IE 5, by selecting Tools and Internet Options. Select the Content tab and click the Enable. When the rating exceeds the defined levels the Content Advisor will block the site. You can set the ratings in Netscape 4.7, by selecting Help and NetWatch. We can use the META tag or the response.PICS property to add a rating to our site.

Syntax
Response. PICS(picslabel)

Parameter	Description
picslabel	A properly formatted PICS label

Examples

For an ASP file that includes:

```
<%
        response.PICS("(PICS-1.1 <http://www.rsac.org/ratingv01.html>
        by " & chr(34) & "your@name.com" & chr(34) &
        " for " & chr(34) & "http://www.somesite.com" & chr(34) &
        " on " & chr(34) & "2002.10.05T02:15-0800" & chr(34) &
        " r (n 2 s 0 v 1 l 2))")
%>
```

the following header would be added:
PICS-label:(PICS-1.1 <http://www.rsac.org/ratingv01.html>
by "your@name.com"
for "http://www.somesite.com"
on "2002.10.05T02:15-0800"
r (n 2 s 0 v 1 l 2))

i. Status

The Status property specifies the value of the status line returned by the server.
Tip: Use this property to modify the status line returned by the server.
Syntax
        response.Status=statusdescription

Parameter	Description
statusdescription	A three-digit number and a description of that code, like

404 Not Found
Note: Status values are defined in the HTTP specification.

Examples

```
<%
        ip=request.ServerVariables("REMOTE_ADDR")
        if ip<>"194.248.333.500" then
                response.Status="401 Unauthorized"
                response.Write(response.Status)
                response.End
        end if
%>
```

Methods

a. AddHeader

The AddHeader method adds a new HTTP header and a value to the HTTP response.
Note: Once a header has been added, it cannot be removed.
In IIS 4.0 you have to call this method before any output is sent to the browser. In IIS 5.0 you can call the AddHeader method at any point in the script, as long as it precedes any calls to the response. Flush method.

Syntax

Response.AddHeader name,value

Parameter	Description
name	Required. The name of the new header variable (cannot contain underscores)
value	Required. The initial value of the new header variable

Examples

<%Response.AddHeader "WARNING","Error message text"%>

b. AppendToLog

The AppendToLog method adds a string to the end of server log entry for this request. You can call this method multiple times in a script. Each time it is called it will append the specified string to the log entry.

Syntax

Response. AppendToLog string

Parameter	Description
string	Required. The text to append to the log file (cant contain any comma)

Examples

<%Response.AppendToLog "My log message"%>

c. BinaryWrite

The BinaryWrite method writes data directly to the output without any character conversion.
Tip: This method is used to write image data (BLOB) from a database to a browser.
Syntax

response.BinaryWrite data

Parameter	Description
data	Required. The binary information to be sent

Examples
Example 1
If you have an object that generates an array of bytes, you can use BinaryWrite to send the bytes to an application:

```
<%
Set objBinaryGen=Server.CreateObject("MyComponents.BinaryGenerator")
pic=objBinaryGen.MakePicture
response.BinaryWrite pic
%>
```

d. Clear

The Clear method clears any buffered HTML output.
Note: This method does not clear the response headers, only the response body. If response. Buffer is false, this method will cause a run-time error.

Syntax
    response.Clear

Examples
```
<% response.Buffer=true %>
<html> <body>
<p>This is some text I want to send to the user.</p>
<p>No, I changed my mind. I want to clear the text.</p>
<% response.Clear %>
</body> </html>
Output:
(nothing)
```

e. End
    The End method stops processing a script, and returns the current result.
Note: This method will flush the buffer if Response.Buffer has been set to true. If you do not want to return any output to the user, you should call Response.Clear first.

Syntax
    Response.End

Examples
```
<html> <body>
<p>I am writing some text. This text will never be
<% Response.End %>
finished! It's too late to write more!</p>
</body> </html>
```

Output:
I am writing some text. This text will never be

f. Flush
    The Flush method sends buffered HTML output immediately.
Note: If response.Buffer is false, this method will cause a run-time error.

Syntax
    Response.Flush
Examples
```
<% Response.Buffer=true %>
    <html> <body>
        <p>I write some text, but I will control when the
        text will be sent to the browser.</p>
        <p>The text is not sent yet. I hold it back!</p>
        <p>OK, let it go!</p>
```

```
<% Response.Flush %>
      </body> </html>
```
Output:
I write some text, but I will control when the
text will be sent to the browser.

The text is not sent yet. I hold it back!

OK, let it go!

g. Write
The Write method writes a specified string to the output.

Syntax
Response. Write variant

Parameter	Description
variant	Required. The data to write

Examples
Example 1
```
<%  Response.Write "Hello World" %>
```

Output:
Hello World

Example 2
```
<%   name="John"
      Response.Write(name)
%>
```
Output: John

Example 3
```
<% Response.Write("Hello<br />World") %>
```
Output:
Hello
World

3. Application object

A group of ASP files that work together to perform some purpose is called an application. The Application object in ASP is used to tie these files together.

The Application object is used to store and access variables from any page, just like the Session object. The difference is that ALL users share one Application object, while with Sessions there is one Session object for EACH user.

The Application object should hold information that will be used by many pages in the application (like database connection information). This means that you can access the information from any page. It also means that you can change the information in one place and the changes will automatically be reflected on all pages.

The Application object's collections, methods, and events are described below:

Collections
a. Contents

The Contents collection contains all the items appended to the application/session through a script command. To remove items from the Contents collection, use the Remove and RemoveAll methods.

Syntax

Application.Contents(Key)

Parameter	Description
key	Required. The name of the item to retrieve

Examples

Example 1
Notice that both name and objtest would be appended to the Contents collection:

```
<%
Application("name")="yahoo"
Set Application("objtest")=Server.CreateObject("ADODB.Connection")
%>
```

Example 2
To loop through the Contents collection:

```
<%
for each x in Application.Contents
      Response.Write(x & "=" & Application.Contents(x) & "<br />")
next
%>
```
or:
```
<%
For i=1 to Application.Contents.Count
```

```
   Response.Write(i & "=" & Application.Contents(i) & "<br />")
Next
%>
```

Example 3

```
<%
        Application("date")="2001/05/05"
        Application("author")="abc"  for each x in Application.Contents
                    Response.Write(x & "=" & Application.Contents(x) & "<br>")
          next
%>
```
Output:
date=2001/05/05
author=abc

b. StaticObjects
        The StaticObjects collection contains all the objects appended to the application/session with the HTML <object> tag.

Syntax
```
        Application.StaticObjects(Key)
        Session.StaticObjects(Key)
```

Parameter	Description
key	Required. The name of the item to retrieve

Examples
Example 1
To loop through the StaticObjects collection:
```
<%
for each x in Application.StaticObjects
        Response.Write(x & "<br />")
next
%>
```

Example 2
In Global.asa:
```
<object runat="server" scope="application" id="MsgBoard"
progid="msgboard.MsgBoard">
</object>
<object runat="server" scope="application" id="AdRot"
progid="MSWC.AdRotator">
</object>
```
In an ASP file:
```
<%
        for each x in Application.StaticObjects
              Response.Write(x & "<br />")
        next
%>
```
Output:

MsgBoard
AdRot

Methods of Contents collection
a. Remove
The Contents.Remove method deletes an item from the Contents collection.

Syntax
Application.Contents.Remove(name|index)

Parameter	Description
name	The name of the item to remove
index	The index of the item to remove

Examples
Example 1
```
<%
        Application("test1")=("First test")
        Application("test2")=("Second test")
        Application("test3")=("Third test")
        Application.Contents.Remove("test2")
        for each x in Application.Contents
                Response.Write(x & "=" & Application.Contents(x) & "<br />")
        next
%>
```
Output:
test1=First test
test3=Third test

Example 2
```
<%
        Application("test1")=("First test")
        Application("test2")=("Second test")
        Application("test3")=("Third test")
        Application.Contents.Remove(2)
        for each x in Application.Contents
                Response.Write(x & "=" & Application.Contents(x) & "<br />")
        next
%>
```

Output:
test1=First test
test3=Third test

b. RemoveAll
The Contents.RemoveAll method deletes all items from the Contents collection.

Syntax

    Application.Contents.RemoveAll()

Example

<% Application.Contents.RemoveAll() %>

Methods of Application object

a. Lock Method

    The Lock method prevents other users from modifying the variables in the Application object.

b. Unlock Method

The Unlock method enables other users to modify the variables stored in the Application object (after it has been locked using the Lock method).

Syntax

    Application.Lock
    Application.Unlock

Examples

The example below uses the Lock method to prevent more than one user from accessing the variable visits at a time, and the Unlock method to unlock the locked object so that the next client can increment the variable visits:

<%

    Application.Lock
            Application("visits")=Application("visits")+1
    Application.Unlock

%>

This page has been visited

<%=Application("visits")%> times!

Events

Application OnStart Event - The Application_OnStart event occurs before the first new session is created (when the Application object is first referenced). This event is placed in the Global.asa

Note: Referencing to a Session, Request, or Response objects in the Application_OnStart event script will cause an error.

Application OnEnd Event -The Application_OnEnd event occurs when the application ends (when the web server stops).

This event is placed in the Global.asa file.

Note: The MapPath method cannot be used in the Application_OnEnd code.

Syntax

<script language="vbscript" runat="server">

    Sub Application_OnStart

        . . .

    End Sub
    Sub Application_OnEnd

        . . .

    End Sub

</script>

Examples

Global.asa:

```
<script language="vbscript" runat="server">
    Sub Application_OnEnd()
        Application("totvisitors")=Application("visitors")
    End Sub
    Sub Application_OnStart
        Application("visitors")=0
    End Sub
    Sub Session_OnStart
        Application.Lock
            Application("visitors")=Application("visitors")+1
        Application.UnLock
    End Sub
    Sub Session_OnEnd
        Application.Lock
        Application("visitors")=Application("visitors")-1
        Application.UnLock
    End Sub
</script>
```

To display the number of current visitors in an ASP file:

```
<html> <body>
<p> There are <%response.write(Application("visitors"))%> online now! </p>
</body> </html>
```

4. Session object

The Session object is used to store information about, or change settings for a user session. Variables stored in the Session object hold information about one single user, and are available to all pages in one application.

When you are working with an application, you open it, do some changes and then you close it. This is much like a Session. The computer knows who you are. It knows when you start the application and when you end. But on the Internet there is one problem: the web server does not know who you are and what you do because the HTTP address doesn't maintain state.

ASP solves this problem by creating a unique cookie for each user. The cookie is sent to the client and it contains information that identifies the user. This interface is called the Session object.

The Session object is used to store information about, or change settings for a user session. Variables stored in the Session object hold information about one single user, and are available to all pages in one application. Common information stored in session variables are name, id, and preferences. The server creates a new Session object for each new user, and destroys the Session object when the session expires.

Collections

a. Contents – (Description is same like Application)
      Session.Contents(Key)

Examples
Example 1
Notice that both name and objtest would be appended to the Contents collection:

```
<%
Session("name")="Hege"
Set Session("objtest")=Server. CreateObject("ADODB.Connection")
%>
```

Example 2
To loop through the Contents collection:

```
<%
for each x in Session.Contents
        Response.Write(x & "=" & Session.Contents(x) & "<br />")
next
%>
```

or:

```
<%
For i=1 to Session.Contents.Count
  Response.Write(i & "=" & Session.Contents(i) & "<br />")
Next
%>
```

Example 3

```
<%
Session("name")="Hege"
Session("date")="2001/05/05"
for each x in Session.Contents
        Response.Write(x & "=" & Session.Contents(x) & "<br />")
next
%>
```

Output:
name=Hege
date=2001/05/05

b. StaticObject

Example 1
To loop through the StaticObjects collection:

```
<%
For each x in Session.StaticObjects
        Response.Write (x & "<br />")
Next
%>
```

Example 2 In Global.asa:
```
<object runat="server" scope="session" id="MsgBoard"
progid="msgboard.MsgBoard">
</object>
<object runat="server" scope="session" id="AdRot"
progid="MSWC.AdRotator">
</object>
```
In an ASP file:
```
<%
      for each x in Session.StaticObjects
            Response.Write(x & "<br />")
      next
%>
```
Output:
MsgBoard
AdRot

Examples
Example 1
```
<%
Session("test1")=("First test")
Session("test2")=("Second test")
Session("test3")=("Third test")
Session.Contents.Remove("test2")
for each x in Session.Contents
      Response.Write(x & "=" & Session.Contents(x) & "<br />")
next
%>
```
Output:
test1=First test
test3=Third test

Example 2
```
<%
Session ("test1")=("First test")
Session ("test2")=("Second test")
Session ("test3")=("Third test")
Session.Contents.Remove (2)
for each x in Session. Contents
      Response.Write (x & "=" & Session.Contents(x) & "<br>")
next
%>
```
Output:
test1=First test
test3=Third test

Methods of contents collection
Session.Contents.Remove (name|index)
Session.Contents.RemoveAll ()

Parameter	Description
name	The name of the item to remove
index	The index of the item to remove

Example for the Session Object
```
<% Session.Contents.RemoveAll () %>
```

Properties
a. CodePage
Used to set / retrieve character set that will be used for displaying special characters.
b. LCID
Allows you to set/retrieve local identifier. This represents how time, numbers & currency are to be displayed.
Ex. <%
```
        Session.LCID=1033
        Response.write "US format:"& now & "-" & formatCurrency (1234.56) &
"<p>"
    %>
```
Can be 2057 for UK, 1049 for Russia, 1032 for Greek.
c. SessionID
To track users/visitors as they travel your site, server places SessionID. This is a random number of type long. It is a read only property. This value is passed back & forth by using cookies. This cannot be a unique number overtime, because when you restart your server, this number may be any number.

d. TimeOut
The session can be end when
1. User closes browser or current site.
2. If user do not make a request for any page within certain time.
TimeOut is read/write property
It is a read/write property which stores, number of minutes that visitors can take between request, in your ASP application.
```
        Session.Timeout=NumMinutes
        Response.write Session.TimeOut
```
When session ends all session variables & objects are released.
Method
a. Abandon – To terminate Session, which immediately terminates session. All session variables & objects will get released & session On_End event occurs.

Events
Session_OnStart, Session_OnEnd

Example
1. Session variables can be created anywhere in ASP page.
```
        <html>
```

```
            <body>
                <%Session("color")="Blue"%>
            </body>
        </html>
Displaying a session variable
        <html>
            <body>
                You like <%Session("color")%>
            </body>
        </html>
```

2. for storing arrays
```
<% color(0)="blue"
    color(1)="white"
    session("favcolor")=color
%>
```

To retrieve colors
```
<% color=session("favcolor")
        Response.write "Color 1-" & color(0)
        Response.write "Color 2-" & color(1)
%>
```

5. Server Object

The ASP Server object is used to access properties and methods on the server.

Properties
1. ScriptTimeout
The ScriptTimeout property sets or returns the maximum number of seconds a script can run before it is terminated.
Syntax - Server.ScriptTimeout[=NumSeconds]

Parameter	Description
NumSeconds	The maximum number of seconds a script can run before the server terminates it. Default is 90 seconds

Examples
Example 1
Set the script timeout:
```
<% Server.ScriptTimeout=200 %>
```

Example 2
Retrieve the current value of the ScriptTimeout property:
```
<% response.write(Server.ScriptTimeout) %>
```

Methods
1. CreateObject – use this method to create all your objects i.e. instance of server component.

The server component can be –

A. Components that come with IIS. Designed to extend what you do with ASP pages.
      Ex.- Browser Capabilities, Ad Rotator, Page Counter etc.

B. Provides some additional functionality to your page but are not designed only for ASP.
      Ex. – MS word, Graph generator

C. The contents that you create for yourself.
      Ex. If you want to create a procedure that is not on server i.e. you want to place code in one place & then use it in variety of locations.

Form – set myobj=Server.CreateObject(nameof appclass)
Ex. – set myobj=Server.CreateObject("adodb.connection")

2. HTMLEncode- applies HTML encoding to specific characters or strings, for representing < > signs.
      ConvertedText = Server.HTMLEncode(TextToConvert)
Ex-
<%Response.write "Question 1" & "<p>"
Response.write Server.HTMLEncode("A. P<B") & "<p>"
Response.write Server.HTMLEncode("B. P>B") & "<p>"
Response.write Server.HTMLEncode("C. P=B") & "<p>"
%>
HTML code will be –
A. P < B <p> B. P > B <p> C. P=B <p>

3. MapPath – Takes a virtual file name or pathname & turns it into a real direct path. You can specify a filename with no directories or virtual path with directory relative to webroot & function will find final file. If file doesn't exist, error will be returned.
Ex. - <% Response.write "Path to parent dir." & "<p>"
Response.write Server.MapPath ("../") & "<p>"
Response.write "Path to current dir." & "<p>"
Response.write Server.MapPath ("./") & "<p>"
Response.write "Path to file in current dir." & "<p>"
Response.write Server.MapPath ("myfile.txt") & "<p>"
Response.write "Path to root dir." & "<p>"
Response.write Server.MapPath ("/") & "<p>" %>

4. URLEncode – This method translates all special characters in a URL into their non-functional equivalents. Mostly used when passing a URL as part of QueryString.
Ex- Response.write Server.URLEncode (http://www.yahoo.com)
Passing will be – http%3A%2F%2Fwww%2Eyahoo%2Ecom

%3A – Colon, %2F – Forward slash, %2E –dot, %3F- ?, + - space, %21 - !
Ex – Response.write Server.URLEncode("Hello?World!") & "<p>"

5. Transfer – Transfers all values of all built-in-objects as well as states of those objects to new page you selected.
Ex – Server.Transfer "part2.asp"

6. Execute – used mostly for subroutine or stored procedure. After calling Execute method on page, that page is executed as part of calling ASP page. You can pass name of procedure you want to call.
Ex. Server.execute "/lib/strfun.asp?name=reverse"
You can't get return value from execute, so put data in session or application variables.

Err Object

Used to determine what error has occurred. Error object is a part of ASP environment so you don't have to use CreateObject method of server to instantiate it.

Properties

1. Number – Returns numeric value corresponding to type of error that has occurred. If no error occurs the value of this property is 0.
2. Description – Displays text message about what error means. But the description is not always meaningful or understandable, to check which error occurs.
3. Source – Name of object or application threw the error.
4. HelpFile – Returns path to help file, if any associated with error number.
5. HelpContext- Returns ID of topic within HelpFile.

Methods

1. Clear – Resets Error object as if an error never occurs.
2. Raise – Provides a way for you to generate your own error.
Form- Err.Raise Number, Source, Description, HelpFile, HelpContext

Error messages & code –
7 – out of memory,   9-subscript out of range
13 – Type mismatch   53 – File not found
58 – File already exists

Debugging your ASP scripts & handling errors –
To reduce bugs count in code, we will need to test the application, searching the bugs. This process of testing to locate bugs is known as debugging.
There are 2 types of bugs-
1. Fatal Bug- Causes to end the execution of program. This is due to defective code. Easy to locate, because when this occurs, ASP scripts stop executing & error message is displayed.
2. Nonfatal Bugs- Are more difficult to locate because there is no error message, but output of code is wrong. The ASP script must be tested for following inputs to locate non-fatal bugs.
    a. Expected input values   b. Near boundary values
    c. Boundary input value   d. Unexpected input value.

Example:
```
<%  Option explicit
     Dim a
          On error resume next
               a=10/0
               If err.number<>0 then
                    Response.write err.description
                    Response.end
               Else
                    Response.write "no problem"
               End if %>
```

Using Database

A database is a collection of organized data, which can be queried & modified. Database can be connected to ASP pages with help of Activex Data Objects (ADOs), component written by Microsoft.

The Open Database Connectivity (ODBC) standard, provides a common interface to a database so that same coed will work regardless of what database we are using.

1. Connection object –

Contains variety of properties & methods for connecting to a database & to manage the behavior of that connection is created using CreateObject method of Server object.

Ex – set con = Server.CreateObject ("adodb.connection")

Properties

1. Attributes – used for some db servers to indicate whether a new transaction should be started after one is complete or aborted. Read/ write property. The values can be –

> 131072 – if you wanted a transaction to start auto. After one completed.
> 262144- if to start transaction after one canceled.

2. CommandTimeOut – to set how long you will allow a command to execute before it times out. Read/write property. Def. is 30 sec.

> Con.CommandTimeOut=numofsec

3. ConnectionString- if you want connection without using DSN, we can supply a connect string that specifies all information ADO needs to connect to db.

> con.ConnectionString=ConnectStringText

In this with driver specify server name, user name, password, name of db in server etc.

Ex- con.ConnectionString="provider=microfsoft.jet.OLEDB.4.0; DataSource='\..\project.mdb'"

Con.open

4. ConnectionTimeOut – To set how long a Connection object should attempt to connect to a db with ConnectionTimeOut property. Read/write property. Default is 15sec.

> Con.ConnectionTimeOut=numsec

5. CursorLocation – stores where the data in a recordset will be located. Read/write property.

> Con.cursorlocation=LocationValue
> Values 2- cursor is on server   3 – cursor is on client.

6. DefaultDatabase – indicates name of db opened through Open method.

> Dbname=con.DefaultDatabase

Ex. - <% set con=Server.CreateObject("adodb.connection")

> Con.open "mydsn","sa","pass"
> Response.write "the default db" & con.DefaultDatabase
> Con.close %>

7. Mode- to indicate how db should be opened. Read, write or both. It is Read-write property.

    Con.mode=value

    1- Read only, 2- write only, 3- read/write

8. Provider – indicates db service used to connect to db Provider=con.provider

9. state – indicates whether connection is opened or closed. 1- open, 0- closed.   Value=con.state

Methods
Allows you to open & manage connections-

1. BeginTrans – Indicates that you want to start a transaction

    con.BeginTrans

2. CommitTrans – Changes are made to db from buffer

    con.CommitTrans

3. RollBackTrans – discards any changes in buffer that are made within scope of current transaction.

    Con.RollBackTrans

4. Close – Provides mechanism for disconnecting a connection object from a db.

    Con.close

5. Open – used to open a connection to db.

    Con.open DSN, username, password, options.

6. Execute – runs a query, stored procedure or some other db functions. Can return nothing or may return recordset.

2. RecordSet object
Used to browse through data returned from Execute method of Connection

        object.

fsEx- set rs = con.execute ("select * from emp")

There are 3 regions of recordset – BOF, records, EOF

If r.s has no records, record pointer will be pointed to both BOF & EOF

Properties
A page is one or more records & that division is carried out through all records

        in recordset.

So if page size is 4 & you have 25 records then you have 7 pages of data.

To handle pages 3 properties are –

1. AbsolutePage – used to jump to specific page or to report what is the

        current page no.

          rs.AbsolutePage = pgnumber or   pgnumber=

        rs.AbsolutePage

2. PageSize – to set or retrieve number of records on page.

          Rs.pageSize=pgsize   Or   pgsize=rs.PageSize

3. PageCount – to find out how many pages there are in RecordSet. This is readonly property
        pgcnt=rs.PageCount

4. AbsolutePosition – Returns exact position of current record.
        Theposition= rs.AbsolutePosition

5. ActiveConnection – to retrieve information about how connection was made.
        Coninfo=rs.ActiveConnection

6. BOF – Reports you, whether you are on beginning of file region.

7. EOF - Reports you, whether you are at end of file region.

8. BookMark – To point to specific record in recordset. Read/write property.
        Rs.BookMark = mybm   or   mybm=Rs.BookMark

9. CacheSize – To set number of records retrieved at one time. Read/write property. Def. is 1.
        Rs.CacheSize = value   or value = rs.CacheSize

10. CursorLocation – sets location of data in recordset

11. CursorType – To specify type of cursor used in rs.
        Rs.CursorType = value
The values are
        0 – adOpenForwardOnly – Default.
        1 – adOpenKeySet – allows free movement through rs. Can see changes & deletes made by users, but doesn't show addition made by other users with refreshing rs.
        2 – adOpenDynamic – allows full movement. Others can see additions, edits, deletions made.
        3 – adOpenStatic – Fully scrollable but disconnects from server after record set is retrivied. Additions, edits, deletes made by other users are not available.

12. EditMode – Returns modification mode, that the record set in.
        m=rs.editmode
        the options are –
        0 – No edit or add mode.
        1 - Current record is in edit mode & changes have not been saved yet.
        2 - Record is in add mode.
        4 - Record has been deleted.

13. You can supply where & order by clause to an open Record set with Filter & Sort properties.
a. Filter – Allows you to supply a field name & condition for field.

RS.Filter = FilterText

Example:
rsRecordSet.Filter = " FirstName = ' Wilma' OR FirstName = 'Betty' "
or
rsRecordSet.Filter = " LastName LIKE F* "
or
rsRecordSet.Filter = " Date >= #12/25/2001# "
or
rsRecordSet.Filter = " Cost > $100.00 AND Cost < $200.00 "

b. Sort – Allows you to supply a field or fields by which you want the records in an open   Recordset sorted.
RS.sort=SortText

14. LockType- DB provider does this to protect more than one person from editing same records.
        RS.LockType = LockValue
1- records in record set are read only.   - adLockReadOnly

2- Record is locked when it is first edited.   - adLockPessimistic

3- Record is locked while it is updating with call using Update method. – adLockOptimistic

15. Source – Returns SQL stmt. Used to generate records in a record set object.

        SQLText = RS.source

Methods –
1. Open – used to open a record set. The form of open method is -
        RS.open SQLText, ConnectString, CursorType, LockType, Options
[Options is an optional parameter that tells the provider how to evaluate source parameter – the values are –
        1. adCmdText- indicates that the provider should evaluate source as a textual definition of command.
        2. adCmdTale – provider should evaluate source as table name.
        3. adCmdStoredProc – source as a stored procedure
2. Supports – used to determine if RecordSet object supports a certain type of functionality. Returns Boolean expression indicating whether the RecordSet object supports indicated function.
        Set varBoolean=object.Supports(cursoroptions)
        Values for Cursor Options are –
        1. adAddNew – to add new records.
        2. adApproxPosition – You can read & set AbsolutePosition & AbsolutePage properties.

3. adBookMark – to access specific record.
4. adDelete   5. adUpdate
3. Update- used to save any changes that you made to current RecordSet.
Object.update [Fieldlist][,valuelist]
4. UpdateBatch – used to save all changes that you made to records in RecordSet object.
Object.UpdateBatch [AffectedRecords]

ADO Command Object

The ADO **Command** object is used to submit and execute a specific (single) query against a database.
The query can command a variety of actions, such as adding, creating, deleting, retrieving, or updating databases (record sets).

Command Objects Properties

ActiveConnection

Used to indicate the specific **Connection** object with which the **Command** object is to be associated and will use for execution.

Code:

Set objCommand.ActiveConnection =
    "Provider=Microsoft.Jet.OLEDB.4.0; Data Source=test.mdb"
orobjConnection.Open "Provider=Microsoft.Jet.OLEDB.4.0; Data Source=test.mdb"
Set objCommand.ActiveConnection = objConnecion

Example:

```
<%
        set conn=server.createobject("adodb.connection")
        conn.open "mydsn"
        set cmd=server.createobject("adodb.command")
        set cmd.activeconnection=conn
cmd.commandtext="select count(empid) as cnt from emp where deptno=1"
set rs=cmd.execute
Response.write "total number of employees working in dept 1 are" & rs("cnt")
%>
```

The #include directive is used to create functions, headers, footers, or elements that will be reused on multiple pages.

The #include Directive

You can insert the content of one ASP file into another ASP file before the server executes it, with the #include directive. The #include directive is used to create functions, headers, footers, or elements that will be reused on multiple pages.

How to Use the #include Directive
Here is a file called "mypage.asp":

```
<html> <body>
<h3>Words of Wisdom:</h3>
<p><!--#include file="wisdom.inc"--></p>
<h3>The time is:</h3>
<p><!--#include file="time.inc"--></p>
</body> </html>
```

Here is the "wisdom.inc" file:

```
"One should never increase, beyond what is necessary,
the number of entities required to explain anything."
```

Here is the "time.inc" file:

```
<% Response.Write(Time) %>
```

If you look at the source code in a browser, it will look something like this:

```
<html> <body>
<h3>Words of Wisdom:</h3>
<p>"One should never increase, beyond what is necessary,
the number of entities required to explain anything."</p>
<h3>The time is:</h3>
<p>11:33:42 AM</p>
</body> </html>
```

Syntax for Including Files

To include a file in an ASP page, place the #include directive inside comment tags:

```
<!--#include virtual="somefilename"-->
```

or

```
<!--#include file ="somefilename"-->
```

The Virtual Keyword

Use the virtual keyword to indicate a path beginning with a virtual directory.
If a file named "header.inc" resides in a virtual directory named /html, the following line would insert the contents of "header.inc":

```
<!-- #include virtual ="/html/header.inc" -->
```

The File Keyword

Use the file keyword to indicate a relative path. A relative path begins with the directory that contains the including file.
If you have a file in the html directory, and the file "header.inc" resides in html\headers, the following line would insert "header.inc" in your file:

```
<!-- #include file ="headers\header.inc" -->
```

Note that the path to the included file (headers\header.inc) is relative to the including file. If the file containing this #include statement is not in the html directory, the statement will not work.

You can also use the file keyword with the syntax (..\) to include a file from a higher-level directory.

Tips and Notes

In the sections above we have used the file extension ".inc" for included files. Notice that if a user tries to browse an INC file directly, its content will be displayed. If your included file contains confidential information or information you do not want any users to see, it is better to use an ASP extension. The source code in an ASP file will not be visible after the interpretation. An included file can also include other files, and one ASP file can include the same file more than once.

Important: Included files are processed and inserted before the scripts are executed.

The following script will not work because ASP executes the #include directive before it assigns a value to the variable:

```
<%
fname="header.inc"
%>
<!--#include file="<%=fname%>"-->
```

You cannot open or close a script delimiter in an INC file. This script will not work:

```
<%
For i = 1 To n
  <!--#include file="count.inc"-->Next %>
```

But this script will work:

```
<% For i = 1 to n %>
<!--#include file="count.inc" -->
<% Next %>
```

The Global.asa file

The Global.asa file is an optional file that can contain declarations of objects, variables, and methods that can be accessed by every page in an ASP application. All valid browser scripts (JavaScript, VBScript, JScript, PerlScript, etc.) can be used within Global.asa.

The Global.asa file can contain only the following:

1. Application events
2. Session events
3. <object> declarations
4. TypeLibrary declarations
5. the #include directive

Note: The Global.asa file must be stored in the root directory of the ASP application, and each application can only have one Global.asa file.

Events in Global.asa

In Global.asa you can tell the application and session objects what to do when the application/session starts and what to do when the application/session ends. The code for this is placed in event handlers. The Global.asa file can contain four types of events:

Application_OnStart - This event occurs when the FIRST user calls the first page from an ASP application. This event occurs after the Web server is restarted or after the Global.asa file is edited. The "Session_OnStart" event occurs immediately after this event.

Session_OnStart - This event occurs EVERY time a NEW user requests his or her first page in the ASP application.

Session_OnEnd - This event occurs EVERY time a user ends a session. A user ends a session after a page has not been requested by the user for a specified time (by default this is 20 minutes).

Application_OnEnd - This event occurs after the LAST user has ended the session. Typically, this event occurs when a Web server stops. This procedure is used to clean up settings after the Application stops, like delete records or write information to text files.

A Global.asa file could look something like this:

```
<script language="vbscript" runat="server">
sub Application_OnStart
""some code
end sub
sub Application_OnEnd
""some code
end sub
sub Session_OnStart
""some code
end sub
sub Session_OnEnd
""some code
end sub
</script>
```

Note: We cannot use the ASP script delimiters (<% and %>) to insert scripts in the Global.asa file, we will have to put the subroutines inside the HTML <script> tag.

<object> Declarations

It is possible to create objects with session or application scope in Global.asa by using the <object> tag.

Note: The <object> tag should be outside the <script> tag!

Syntax

```
<object runat="server" scope="scope" id="id"
{progid="progID"|classid="classID"}>
....
</object>
```

Parameter	Description
scope	Sets the scope of the object (either Session or Application)
id	Specifies a unique id for the object
ProgID	An id associated with a class id. The format for ProgID is Vendor.]Component [.Version] Either ProgID or ClassID must be specified.
ClassID	Specifies a unique id for a COM class object. Either ProgID or ClassID must be specified.

Examples
The example creates an object of session scope named "MyAd" by using the ProgID parameter:

```
<object runat="server" scope="session" id="MyAd"
progid="MSWC.AdRotator">
</object>
```

Restrictions
Restrictions on what you can include in the Global.asa file:
You can not displ y text that is written in the Global.asa file. This file can't display information
You can only use Server and Application objects in the Application_OnStart and Application_OnEnd subroutines. In the Session_OnEnd subroutine, you can use Server, Application, and Session objects. In the Session_OnStart subroutine you can use any built-in object

How to use the Subroutines
Global.asa is often used to initialize variables.
The example below shows how to detect the exact time a visitor first arrives on a Web site. The time is stored in a Session variable named "started", and the value of the "started" variable can be accessed from any ASP page in the application:

```
<script language="vbscript" runat="server">
sub Session_OnStart
Session("started")=now()
end sub
</script>
```

Global.asa can also be used to control page access.
The example below shows how to redirect every new visitor to another page, in this case to a page called "newpage.asp":

```
<script language="vbscript" runat="server">
sub Session_OnStart
    Response.Redirect("newpage.asp")
end sub
</script>
```

And you can include functions in the Global.asa file.

In the example below the Application_OnStart subroutine occurs when the Web server starts. Then the Application_OnStart subroutine calls another subroutine named "getcustomers". The "getcustomers" subroutine opens a database and retrieves a record set from the "customers" table. The record set is assigned to an array, where it can be accessed from any ASP page without querying the database:

```
<script language="vbscript" runat="server">
sub Application_OnStart
getcustomers
end sub
sub getcustomers
set conn=Server.CreateObject("ADODB.Connection")
conn.Provider="Microsoft.Jet.OLEDB.4.0"
```

```
conn.Open "c:/webdata/northwind.mdb"
set rs=conn.execute("select name from customers")
Application("customers")=rs.GetRows
rs.Close
conn.Close
end sub
</script>
```

Global.asa Example
In this example we will create a Global.asa file that counts the number of current visitors.
The Application_OnStart sets the Application variable "visitors" to 0 when the server starts
The Session_OnStart subroutine adds one to the variable "visitors" every time a new visitor arrives
The Session_OnEnd subroutine subtracts one from "visitors" each time this subroutine is triggered
The Global.asa file:

```
<script language="vbscript" runat="server">
Sub Application_OnStart
      Application("visitors")=0
End Sub
Sub Session_OnStart
      Application.Lock
      Application("visitors")=Application("visitors")+1
      Application.UnLock
End Sub
Sub Session_OnEnd
      Application.Lock
      Application("visitors")=Application("visitors")-1
      Application.UnLock
End Sub
</script>
```

To display the number of current visitors in an ASP file:

```
<html><body><p>There are
<%response.write(Application("visitors"))%>
online now!  </p> </body> </html>
```

Collaborative Data Objects for Windows NT server (CDONTS)

CDO is a built-in component in ASP. This component is used to send e-mails with ASP.

Sending e-mail with CDO
CDO (Collaboration Data Objects) is a Microsoft technology that is designed to simplify the creation of messaging applications.
CDO is a built-in component in ASP. We will show you how to use this component to send e-mail with ASP.

How about CDONTs?
CDONTS is designed to run on Windows NT server running IIS 4.0 or later.

Examples using CDO
Sending a text e-mail:

```
<%
Set myMail=CreateObject("CDO.Message")
myMail.Subject="Sending email with CDO"
myMail.From="mymail@mydomain.com"
myMail.To="someone@somedomain.com"
myMail.TextBody="This is a message."
myMail.Send
%>
```

Sending a text e-mail with Bcc and CC fields:

```
<%
Set myMail=CreateObject("CDO.Message")
myMail.Subject="Sending email with CDO"
myMail.From="mymail@mydomain.com"
myMail.To="someone@somedomain.com"
myMail.Bcc="someoneelse@somedomain.com"
myMail.Cc="someoneelse2@somedomain.com"
myMail.TextBody="This is a message."
myMail.Send
%>
```

Sending an HTML e-mail:

```
<%
Set myMail=CreateObject("CDO.Message")
myMail.Subject="Sending email with CDO"
myMail.From="mymail@mydomain.com"
myMail.To="someone@somedomain.com"
myMail.HTMLBody = "<h1>This is a message.</h1>"
myMail.Send
%>
```

Sending an HTML e-mail that sends a webpage from a website:

```
<%
Set myMail=CreateObject("CDO.Message")
myMail.Subject="Sending email with CDO"
myMail.From="mymail@mydomain.com"
myMail.To="someone@somedomain.com"
myMail.CreateMHTMLBody "http://www.w3schools.com/asp/"
myMail.Send
%>
```

Sending an HTML e-mail that sends a webpage from a file on your computer:

```
<%
Set myMail=CreateObject("CDO.Message")
myMail.Subject="Sending email with CDO"
myMail.From="mymail@mydomain.com"
myMail.To="someone@somedomain.com"
myMail.CreateMHTMLBody "file://c:/mydocuments/test.htm"
myMail.Send
%>
```

Sending a text e-mail with an Attachment:

```
<%
Set myMail=CreateObject("CDO.Message")
myMail.Subject="Sending email with CDO"
myMail.From="mymail@mydomain.com"
myMail.To="someone@somedomain.com"
myMail.TextBody="This is a message."
myMail.AddAttachment "c:\mydocuments\test.txt"
myMail.Send
%>
```

Properties

1. **To:**   E-mail addresses of recipients
2. **From:**   E-mail address of sender
3. **Subject:**   Subject of mesg.
4. **Body:**   Text of mail message.
5. **CC:**   Carbon Copy recipients
6. **BCC:**   Blind Carbon Copy recipients
7. **Importance:**   Set the level of importance. 0 - low, 1- Normal (default), 2-high
8. **BodyFormat:**   0- Plain Text 1- HTML
9. **MailFormat:**   0- Text 1- MIME type

Methods:
1. **Send:**   Sends email message
2. **AttachFile:**   Allows you to attach a file to a message.
   Objmail.attachfile filelocation, filename
   Ex: objmail.attachfile "e:\inetpub\logo.gif","company logo"

3. **AttachURL:**   Attach files that are part of an HTML email.

Objects that extends ASP capabilities:
IIS comes with a variety of components that assist in ASP development.

1. Browser Capabilities Component:
Provides you with information about visitors browser & information about their system.

To make the object of this component:
Set bc=server.createobject ("MSWC.BrowserType")

Poperties:
1. **Browser:**   returns name of browser the client using.
2. **Version**
3. **Platform:**   returns name of OS the client using.
4. **Frames:**   returns whether clients browser supports frames or not.

The following properties returns true or false, as per browsers settings on client side.

5. **Tables**   6. **Cookies**
7. **vbscript**   8. **javascript**
9. **javaapplets**   10. **Activexcontrols**

Modifying Browser.INI file
- Its just a text file, that must be in specified format.

Example:
[MyBrowser 1.0]
browser=MyBrowser
version=1.0
frames=false
tables=True .....

2. AD Rotator Component:
- Gives a tool to manage the banner ads, that appear on web page.
- The component will randomly display a banner ad on ASP page each time the page is accessed.
- It has a separate schedule file to determine how often to display one banner ad vs another.

Set objadrot=server.createobjcet("MSWC.AdRotaotr")

The GetAdvertisement method is called to retrive information about the banner ad to be displayed. This method is paased a single parameter, the Path to scheduile file, which contains list of banner ads that are to be displayed & how often they are to be displayed.

```
Set objadrot=server.createobjcet("MSWC.AdRotaotr")
Response.write objadrot.GetAdvertisement("/adfiles/adfile.txt")
```

Ex: the contents of schedule file with name: adfile.txt

Redirect http://www.abcd.com/html/adfiles/adRedirect.asp
Width 468
Height 60
Border=0
*
http://www.abcd.com/ html/adfiles/ha.gif
http://www.abcd.com/html/adfiles/ha.html
Get Your organization Online
10
http://www.abcd.com/ html/adfiles/sgianim.gif
http://www.silkgraph.com
Silkscreen Graphics Inc.
10
http://www.abcd.com/ html/adfiles/forrent.gif
mailto:abcd@ibm.net
Space for rent.
10

The 1st section of schedule file contains configuration information. The 1st line contains page to go to when visitors click on banner ad.

The 2nd & 3rd lines of first section contains width & height of banner ad with border.

After *
The 1st line for each of the banner ad's entries is the path to banner ad.
The 2nd line is web location that visitors should eventually be redirected to when thjey click on banner ad.
The 3rd line is alternative text.
The 4th line contains proportional amount that this banner ad should displayed vs other banner ads.

To call these ads create an ASP page with name adRedirect.asp
```
<%
      Response.Redirect(request.queryString("url"))
%>
```

3. Page Counter Component
- Provides a way to track & display the number of hits on a web page.
- It is a part of IIS resource kit.

Set mypagecnt=server. CreateObject("MSWC.PageCounter")

Example:
```
<%
Set mypagecnt=server. CreateObject("MSWC.PageCounter")
mypagecnt.pagehit        'method of pagecounter to increase the count for
                         'particular page
response.write mypagecnt.hits              ' to display counter.
%>
```

4. Content Linking Component
- Provides a way for you to link pages that are to be viewed in a series, pages that have sequential meaning.

Set MyCl=Server.createObject("MSWC.NextLink")

Create a text file of the index:
Example
Get_method.asp Get Method
set_method.asp set Method
increment_method.asp Increment Method

Method	Purpose
GetListCount	Ret. No. Of entries in a index file.
GetListIndex	Ret. The numeric position of the current page in the index file.
GetNextURL	Ret. The URL of the next page
GetNextDescription	Ret. The description of the next page
GetPreviousURL	
GetPreviousDescription	
GetNthURL	
GetNthDescription	

For all of these methods pass name of txt file as argument.

Ex:
Response.write mycl.getListCount("clist.txt")

Example:
```
Set MyCl=Server.createObject("MSWC.NextLink")
Cnt=MyCl.GetListCount("clist.txt")
<%for i=1 to cnt %>
<tr>
<td> <a href="<%response.write MyCl.GetNthURL("clist.txt",i)%>">
Response.write MyCl.GetNthDescription("clist.txt",i)%></a>
```

```
</td>
</tr>
<%Next%>
```

5. Content Rotator Component

- Provides a way to have different content appear on pages whenever page is loaded.
- Part of IIS resource Kit with name contort.dll

Set objcr=Server.createObject("IISSample.ContentRotator")

The content schedular text file may contain:
```
%% #2
<b><font name="Arial">
Live all your days like they are your first day & your last.
</font></b>

%% #3
<i><font name="Arial">
Hello & Welcome!!!
</font></i>

%% #1               //lowest value
<b><font name="Arial">
Think Positive
</font></b>
```

[the 1st entry has a ranking of 2, if weadd nos we get 6. i.e. 2/6 or 33 percent chance of being viewed.]

```
Ex:
<% Set objcr=Server.createObject("IISSample.ContentRotator")
if isEmpty(request.QueryString("Show")) then
      response.write objcr.ChooseContent("cr.txt")
else
      objcr.GetAllContent("cr.txt")
end if %>
```

ChooseContent()- to display a single quote.
ChooseAllContent()- to write all contents to browser.

6.MyInfo Component

- is made up of properties that you create just by setting their values & retrieve just by specifying their name

Example:
```
<%
    Set MyInf=Server.CreateObject("MSWC.MyInfo")
    MyInf.companyname="ABC Company"
    MyInf.address="Nigdi, Pune" %>
```

Once the component is created, you can create & access properties as you like.
```
<%
    Set MyInf=Server.CreateObject("MSWC.MyInfo")
    Response.write "<b>This is from different ASP page Application" &
    MyInf.companyname &"located at:" & MyInf.address
%>
```

7. Counters Component

- Provides a simple interface to store integers that you can read, write, remove & increment across all the pages in your site & across the boundaries of ASP applications.

Example:
```
<%
set cnt=server.createobject("MSWC.Counters")
cnt.set  "pgcnt", 1

cnt.Increment "pgcnt"            ' to increment

cnt.Remove "pgcnt"              ' to remove

Response.write "a counter value:" & cnt.get("pgcnt")          ' to display.

%>
```

ASP FileSystemObject Object

The FileSystemObject object is used to access the file system on the server.

Examples
1. Does a specified file exist?

```
<html> <body>
<% Set fs=Server.CreateObject("Scripting.FileSystemObject")
If (fs.FileExists("c:\winnt\cursors\3dgarro.cur"))=true Then
    Response.Write("File c:\winnt\cursors\3dgarro.cur exists.")
Else
    Response.Write("File c:\winnt\cursors\3dgarro.cur does not exist.")
End If
set fs=nothing %>
</body> </html>
```

The FileSystemObject Object
The FileSystemObject object is used to access the file system on the server. This object can manipulate files, folders, and directory paths. It is also possible to retrieve file system information with this object.
The following code creates a text file (c:\test.txt) and then writes some text to the file:

```
<%
dim fs,fname
set fs=Server.CreateObject("Scripting.FileSystemObject")
set fname=fs.CreateTextFile("c:\test.txt",true)
fname.WriteLine("Hello World!")
fname.Close
set fname=nothing
set fs=nothing
%>
```

The FileSystemObject object's properties and methods are described below:
Properties
Drives Property
The Drives property returns a collection of all Drive objects on the computer.
Syntax

    [drivecoll=]FileSystemObject.Drives

Methods
1. The **BuildPath** Method
The BuildPath method appends a name to an existing path.
Syntax - [newpath=]FileSystemObject.BuildPath(path,name)

Parameter	Description
path	Required. The path to append a name to
name	Required. The name to append to the path

Example

```
<%
dim fs,path
set fs=Server.CreateObject("Scripting.FileSystemObject")
path=fs.BuildPath("c:\mydocuments","test")
response.write(path)
set fs=nothing
%>
Output:
c:\mydocuments\test
```

2. The **CopyFile** Method

The CopyFile method copies one or more files from one location to another.

Syntax - FileSystemObject.CopyFile source,destination[,overwrite]

Parameter	Description
source	Required. The file or files to copy (wildcards can be used}
destination	Required. Where to copy the file or files (wildcards cannot be used}
overwrite	Optional. A Boolean value that specifies whether an existing file can be overwritten. True allows existing files to be overwritten and False prevents existing files from being overwritten. Default is True

Example
```
<%
dim fs
set fs=Server.CreateObject("Scripting.FileSystemObject")
fs.CopyFile "c:\mydocuments\web\*.htm","c:\webpages\"
set fs=nothing
%>
```

3. The **CopyFolder** Method

The CopyFolder method copies one or more folders from one location to another.

Syntax - FileSystemObject.CopyFolder source,destination[,overwrite]

Parameter	Description
source	Required. The folder or folders to copy (wildcards can be used)
destination	Required. Where to copy the folder or folders (wildcards cannot be used)
overwrite	Optional. A Boolean value that indicates whether an existing folder can be overwritten. True allows existing folders to be overwritten and False prevents existing folders from being overwritten. Default is True

Examples
```
<% 'copy all the folders in c:\mydocuments\web to the folder c:\webpages
```

```
dim fs
set fs=Server.CreateObject("Scripting.FileSystemObject")
fs.CopyFolder "c:\mydocuments\web\*","c:\webpages\"
set fs=nothing
%>
<% 'copy only the folder test from c:\mydocuments\web 'to the folder
c:\webpages
dim fs
set fs=Server.CreateObject("Scripting.FileSystemObject")
fs.CopyFolder "c:\mydocuments\web\test","c:\webpages\"
set fs=nothing
%>
```

3. The **CreateFolder** Method
The CreateFolder method creates a new folder.

Syntax - FileSystemObject.CreateFolder(name)

Parameter	Description
name	Required. The name of the folder to create

Example
```
<%
dim fs,f
set fs=Server.CreateObject("Scripting.FileSystemObject")
set f=fs.CreateFolder("c:\asp")
set f=nothing
set fs=nothing
%>
```

5. The **CreateTextFile** Method
The CreateTextFile method creates a new text file in the current folder and returns a TextStream object that can be used to read from, or write to the file.

Syntax
```
FileSystemObject.CreateTextFile(filename[,overwrite[,unicode]])
FolderObject.CreateTextFile(filename[,overwrite[,unicode]])
```

Parameter	Description
filename	Required. The name of the file to create
overwrite	Optional. A Boolean value that indicates whether an existing file can be overwritten. True indicates that the file can be overwritten and False indicates that the file can not be overwritten. Default is True
unicode	Optional. A Boolean value that indicates whether the file is created as a Unicode or an ASCII file. True indicates that the file is created as a Unicode file, False indicates that the file is created as an ASCII file. Default is False

Example for the FileSystemObject object

```
<%
dim fs,tfile
set fs=Server.CreateObject("Scripting.FileSystemObject")
set tfile=fs.CreateTextFile("c:\somefile.txt")
tfile.WriteLine("Hello World!")
tfile.close
set tfile=nothing
set fs=nothing
%>
```

Example for the Folder object
```
<%
dim fs,fo,tfile
Set fs=Server.CreateObject("Scripting.FileSystemObject")
Set fo=fs.GetFolder("c:\test")
Set tfile=fo.CreateTextFile("test.txt",false)
tfile.WriteLine("Hello World!")
tfile.Close
set tfile=nothing
set fo=nothing
set fs=nothing
%>
```

6. The **DeleteFile** Method

The DeleteFile method deletes one or more specified files.
Note: An error will occur if you try to delete a file that doesn't exist.

Syntax - FileSystemObject.DeleteFile(filename[,force])

Parameter	Description
filename	Required. The name of the file or files to delete (Wildcards are allowed)
force	Optional. A Boolean value that indicates whether read-only files will be deleted. True indicates that the read-only files will be deleted, False indicates that they will not be deleted. Default is False

Example
```
<%
dim fs
Set fs=Server.CreateObject("Scripting.FileSystemObject")
fs.CreateTextFile("c:\test.txt",True)
if fs.FileExists("c:\test.txt") then
  fs.DeleteFile("c:\test.txt")
end if
set fs=nothing
%>
```

6. The **DeleteFolder** Method

The DeleteFolder method deletes one or more specified folders.
Note: An error will occur if you try to delete a folder that does not exist.

Syntax - FileSystemObject.DeleteFolder(foldername[,force])

Parameter   **Description**
foldername   Required. The name of the folder or folders to delete
(Wildcards are allowed)
force   Optional. A Boolean value that indicates whether read-only
                   folders will be deleted. True indicates that read-only folders
                   will be deleted, False indicates that they will not be deleted.
                   Default is False

Example
```
<%
dim fs
set fs=Server.CreateObject("Scripting.FileSystemObject")
if fs.FolderExists("c:\temp") then
  fs.DeleteFolder("c:\temp")
end if
set fs=nothing
%>
```

7. The **DriveExists** Method
The DriveExists method returns a Boolean value that indicates whether a
specified drive exists. It returns True if the drive exists and False if not.

Syntax - FileSystemObject.DriveExists(drive)

Parameter   **Description**
drive   Required. A drive letter or a complete path specification

Example
```
<%
dim fs
set fs=Server.CreateObject("Scripting.FileSystemObject")
if fs.DriveExists("c:")=true then
  response.write("Drive c: exists!")
else
  response.write("Drive c: does not exist.")
end If
set fs=nothing
%>
```

8. The **FileExists** Method
The FileExists method returns a Boolean value that indicates whether a
specified file exists. It returns True if the file exists and False if not.
Syntax - FileSystemObject.FileExists(filename)

Parameter   **Description**
filename   Required. The name of the file to check if exist

Example
```
<%
dim fs
set fs=Server.CreateObject("Scripting.FileSystemObject")
if fs.FileExists("c:\asp\introduction.asp")=true then
  response.write("File c:\asp\introduction.asp exists!")
else
  response.write("File c:\asp\introduction.asp does not exist!")
end if
set fs=nothing   %>
```

9. The **FolderExists** Method

The FolderExists method returns a Boolean value that indicates whether a specified folder exists. It returns True if the folder exists and False if not.

Syntax FileSystemObject.FolderExists(foldername)

Parameter Description

foldername Required. The name of the folder to check if exist

Example
```
<%
dim fs
set fs=Server.CreateObject("Scripting.FileSystemObject")
if fs.FolderExists("c:\asp")=true then
  response.write("Folder c:\asp exists!")
else
  response.write("Folder c:\asp does not exist!")
end if
set fs=nothing
%>
```

10. The **GetAbsolutePathName** Method

The GetAbsolutePathName method returns the complete path from the root of the drive for the specified path.

Syntax - FileSystemObject.GetAbsolutePathName(path)

Parameter   **Description**

path   Required. The path to change to a complete path

Examples
Assume that the current directory is c:\temp\test:
Example 1
```
<%
dim fs,path
set fs=Server.CreateObject("Scripting.FileSystemObject")
```

```
path=fs.GetAbsolutePathName("c:")
response.write(path)
%>
Output:
c:\temp\test
```
Example 2
```
<%
dim fs,path
set fs=Server.CreateObject("Scripting.FileSystemObject")
path=fs.GetAbsolutePathName("mydoc.txt")
response.write(path)
%>
Output:
c:\temp\test\mydoc.txt
```

Example 3
```
<%
dim fs,path
set fs=Server.CreateObject("Scripting.FileSystemObject")
path=fs.GetAbsolutePathName("private\mydoc.txt")
response.write(path)
%>
Output:
c:\temp\test\private\mydoc.txt
```

11. The GetBaseName Method
The GetBaseName method returns the base name of a file or folder in the specified path.

Syntax - FileSystemObject.GetBaseName(path)

Parameter	Description
path	Required. The path for the file or folder whose base name is to be returned

Example
```
<%
dim fs
set fs=Server.CreateObject("Scripting.FileSystemObject")
Response.Write(fs.GetBaseName("c:\winnt\cursors\3dgarro.cur"))
set fs=nothing
%>
Output:
3dgarro
```

12. The GetDrive Method
The GetDrive method returns a Drive object that is specified by the drivespec parameter.

Syntax - FileSystemObject.GetDrive(drivespec)

Parameter	Description
drivespec	Required. Can be a drive letter (c), or a drive letter followed by a colon (c:), or a drive letter followed by a colon and path separator (c:\), or any network share specification (\\computer2\share1)

Example
```
<%
dim fs,d
set fs=Server.CreateObject("Scripting.FileSystemObject")
set d=fs.GetDrive("c:\")
set fs=nothing
%>
```

13. The GetDriveName Method

The GetDriveName method returns a string that contains the drive name of the specified path.

Syntax - FileSystemObject.GetDriveName(path)

Parameter	Description
path	Required. The path that will return a drive name

Example
```
<%
dim fs,dname
set fs=Server.CreateObject("Scripting.FileSystemObject")
dname=fs.GetDriveName("c:\test\test.htm")
Response.Write(dname)
set fs=nothing
%>
Output:
c:
```

14. The GetExtensionName Method

The GetExtensionName method returns a string that contains the file extension name for the last component in a specified path.

Syntax - FileSystemObject.GetExtensionName(path)

Parameter	Description
path	Required. The path for the file whose file extension name is to be returned

Example
```
<% dim fs
set fs=Server.CreateObject("Scripting.FileSystemObject")
Response.Write(fs.GetExtensionName("c:\test\test.htm"))
set fs=nothing %>
```

Output: htm

15. The GetFile Method
The GetFile method returns a File object for the specified path.

Syntax - FileSystemObject.GetFile(path)

Parameter	Description
path	Required. The path to a specific file

Example
```
<%
dim fs,f
set fs=Server.CreateObject("Scripting.FileSystemObject")
set f=fs.GetFile("c:\test\test.htm")
Response.Write("The file was last modified on: ")
Response.Write(f.DateLastModified)
set f=nothing
set fs=nothing
%>
Output:
The file was last modified on 01/01/20 4:23:56 AM
```

16. The GetFileName Method
The GetFileName method returns a string that contains the file name or folder name for the last component in a specified path.

Syntax - FileSystemObject.GetFileName(path)

Examples
```
<%
dim fs,p
set fs=Server.CreateObject("Scripting.FileSystemObject")
p=fs.getfilename("c:\test\test.htm")
response.write(p)
set fs=nothing
%>
```
Output:
test.htm
```
<%
dim fs,p
set fs=Server.CreateObject("Scripting.FileSystemObject")
p=fs.getfilename("c:\test\")
response.write(p)
set fs=nothing
%>
```
Output: test

18. The GetFolder Method
The GetFolder method returns a Folder object for the specified path.

Syntax - FileSystemObject.GetFolder(path)

```
<%
dim fs,f
set fs=Server.CreateObject("Scripting.FileSystemObject")
set f=fs.GetFolder("c:\test\")
Response.Write("The folder was last modified on: ")
Response.Write(f.DateLastModified)
set f=nothing
set fs=nothing
%>
Output: The folder was last modified on 01/01/20 4:23:56 AM
```

19. The **GetParentFolderName** Method
The GetParentFolderName method returns the name of the parent folder of the last component in the specified path.

Syntax - FileSystemObject.GetParentFolderName(path)

Example
```
<%
dim fs,p
set fs=Server.CreateObject("Scripting.FileSystemObject")
p=fs.GetParentFolderName("c:\winnt\cursors\3dgarro.cur")
Response.Write(p)
set fs=nothing
%>
Output: cursors\
```

20. The **GetSpecialFolder** Method
The GetSpecialFolder method returns the path to some of Windows' special folders.

Syntax - FileSystemObject.GetSpecialFolder(foldername)

Parameter	Description
foldername	Required. The folder to be returned.
	0=WindowsFolder - Contains files installed by the Windows operating system
	1=SystemFolder - Contains libraries, fonts, and device drivers
	2=TemporaryFolder - Used to store temporary files

Example
```
<%
dim fs,p
set fs=Server.CreateObject("Scripting.FileSystemObject")
set p=fs.GetSpecialFolder(1)
Response.Write(p)
set p=nothing
```

```
set fs=nothing
%>
```
Output: C:\WINNT\system32

21. The **GetTempName** Method
The GetTempName method returns a randomly generated temporary file or folder.

Syntax - FileSystemObject.GetTempName

Example
```
<%
dim fs,tfolder,tname, tfile
Set fs=Server.CreateObject("Scripting.FileSystemObject")
Set tfolder=fs.GetSpecialFolder(2)
tname=fs.GetTempName
Set tfile=tfolder.CreateTextFile(tname)
Response.write (tfile)
%>
```
Output: trb2007.tmp

22. The **MoveFile** Method
The MoveFile method moves one or more files from one location to another.

Syntax - FileSystemObject.MoveFile source,destination

Parameter	Description
source	Required. The path to the file/files to be moved. Can contain wildcard characters in the last component.
destination	Required. Where to move the file/files. Cannot contain wildcard characters

Example
```
<%
dim fs
set fs=Server.CreateObject("Scripting.FileSystemObject")
fs.MoveFile "c:\web\*.gif","c:\images\"
set fs=nothing
%>
```

23. The **MoveFolder** Method
The MoveFolder method moves one or more folders from one location to another.

Syntax - FileSystemObject.MoveFolder source,destination

Parameter	Description
source	Required. The path to the folder/folders to be moved. Can contain wildcard characters in the last component.

destination	Required. Where to move the folder/folders. Cannot contain wildcard characters

Example
```
<%

set fs=Server.CreateObject("Scripting.FileSystemObject")
fs.MoveFolder "c:\test\web\","c:\windows\"
set fs=nothing
%>
```

24. The **OpenTextFile** Method
The OpenTextFile method opens a specified file and returns a TextStream object that can be used to access the file.

Syntax- FileSystemObject.OpenTextFile(fname,mode,create,format)

Parameter	Description
fname	Required. The name of the file to open mode Optional. How to open the file
	1=ForReading - Open a file for reading. You cannot write to this file.
	2=ForWriting - Open a file for writing.
	8=ForAppending - Open a file and write to the end of the file.
create	Optional. Sets whether a new file can be created if the filename does not exist. True indicates that a new file can be created, and False indicates that a new file will not be created. False is default
format	Optional. The format of the file
	0=TristateFalse - Open the file as ASCII. This is default.
	-1=TristateTrue - Open the file as Unicode.
	-2=TristateUseDefault - Open the file using the system default.

Example
```
<%
dim fs,f
set fs=Server.CreateObject("Scripting.FileSystemObject")
set f=fs.OpenTextFile(Server.MapPath("testread.txt"),8,true)
f.WriteLine("This text will be added to the end of file")
f.Close
set f=Nothing
set fs=Nothing
%>
```

The Drive Object
      The Drive object is used to return information about a local disk drive or a network share. The Drive object can return information about a drive's type of file system, free space, serial number, volume name, and more.
Note: You cannot return information about a drive's content with the Drive object. For this purpose you will have to use the Folder object.
      To work with the properties of the Drive object, you will have to create an instance of the Drive object through the FileSystemObject object. First; create a FileSystemObject object and then instantiate the Drive object through the GetDrive method or the Drives property of the FileSystemObject object. The following example uses the GetDrive method of the FileSystemObject object to instantiate the Drive object and the TotalSize property to return the total size in bytes of the specified drive (c:):

```
<%
Dim fs,d
Set fs=Server.CreateObject("Scripting.FileSystemObject")
Set d=fs.GetDrive("c:")
Response.Write("Drive " & d & ":")
Response.Write("Total size in bytes: " & d.TotalSize)
set d=nothing
set fs=nothing
%>
Output: Drive c: Total size in bytes: 4293563392
```

The Drive object's properties are described below:

Properties
1. The **AvailableSpace** Property
The AvailableSpace property returns the amount of available space to a user on the specified drive or network share.
Note: The value returned is often equal to the value returned by the FreeSpace property.
Syntax- DriveObject.AvailableSpace

Example
```
<%
Dim fs,d
Set fs=Server.CreateObject("Scripting.FileSystemObject")
Set d=fs.GetDrive ("c:")
Response.Write ("Drive " & d)
Response.Write (" Available space in bytes: " & d.AvailableSpace)
set d=nothing
set fs=nothing
%>
Output: Drive c: Available space in bytes: 884465152
```

2. The **DriveLetter** Property
The DriveLetter property returns one uppercase letter that identifies the local drive or a network share.

Syntax - DriveObject.DriveLetter
Example
```
<%
dim fs,d
set fs=Server.CreateObject("Scripting.FileSystemObject")
set d=fs.GetDrive("c:")
Response.Write("The drive letter is: " & d.driveletter)
set d=nothing
set fs=nothing
%>
```
Output: The drive letter is: C

3. The **DriveType** Property

The DriveType property returns a value that indicates the type of a specified drive.
This property can return one of the following values:
0 = unknown
1 = removable
2 = fixed
3 = network
4 = CD-ROM
5 = RAM disk

Syntax- DriveObject.DriveType
Example
```
<%
dim fs,d
set fs=Server.CreateObject("Scripting.FileSystemObject")
set d=fs.GetDrive("a:")
Response.Write("The drive type is: " & d.DriveType)
set d=nothing
set fs=nothing
%>
```
Output: The drive type is: 1

4. The **FileSystem** Property

The FileSystem property returns the file system in use for a specified drive.
This property will return one of the following:
FAT - for removable drives
CDFS - for CD-ROM drives
FAT, FAT32 or NTFS - for hard disks on Windows 2000 or Windows NT
FAT or FAT32 - for hard disks on Windows 9x

Syntax - DriveObject.FileSystem
Example
```
<%
dim fs,d
set fs=Server.CreateObject("Scripting.FileSystemObject")
set d=fs.GetDrive("c:")
Response.Write("The file system in use is: " & d.FileSystem)
```

```
    set d=nothing
    set fs=nothing
    %>
    Output: The file system in use is: FAT
```

5. The **FreeSpace** Property
The FreeSpace property returns the amount of free space to a user on the specified drive or network share.
Note: The value returned is often equal to the value returned by the AvailableSpace property.
Syntax - DriveObject.FreeSpace
Example
```
<%
dim fs,d
set fs=Server.CreateObject("Scripting.FileSystemObject")
set d=fs.GetDrive("c:")
Response.Write("Drive " & d)
Response.Write(" Free space in bytes: " & d.FreeSpace)
set d=nothing
set fs=nothing
%>
```
Output: Drive c: Free space in bytes: 884465664

6. The **IsReady** Property
The IsReady property returns true if a specified drive is ready and false if not.
Syntax- DriveObject.IsReady
Example
```
        <%
                dim fs,d,n
                set fs=Server.CreateObject("Scripting.FileSystemObject")
                set d=fs.GetDrive("a:")
                n = "The " & d.DriveLetter
                if d.IsReady=true then
                  n=n & " drive is ready!"
                else
                  n=n & " drive is not ready!"
                end if
                Response.Write(n)
                set d=nothing
                set fs=nothing
        %>
```
Output: The A drive is not ready!

7. The **Path** Property
The Path property is used to return the path for a specified drive, file, or folder.
Syntax - DriveObject.Path

Example for the Drive object
```
<%
```

```
        dim fs,d
        set fs=Server.CreateObject("Scripting.FileSystemObject")
        set d=fs.GetDrive("c:")
        Response.Write("The path is " & d.Path)
        set d=nothing
        set fs=nothing
%>
```
Output: The path is C:

Example for the File object
```
<%
        dim fs,f
        set fs=Server.CreateObject("Scripting.FileSystemObject")
        set f=fs.GetFile("c:\asp\test\test.asp")
        Response.Write("The path is: " & f.Path)
        set f=nothing
        set fs=nothing
%>
```
Output: The path is: C:\asp\test\test.asp

Example for the Folder object
```
<%
        dim fs,fo
        set fs=Server.CreateObject("Scripting.FileSystemObject")
        set fo=fs.GetFolder("c:\asp\test")
        Response.Write("The path is: " & fo.Path)
        set fo=nothing
        set fs=nothing
%>
```
Output: The path is: C:\asp\test

7. The **RootFolder** Property
The RootFolder property returns a Folder object that represents the root folder of a specified drive.
Syntax - DriveObject.RootFolder

Example
```
<%
        dim fs,d
        set fs=Server.CreateObject("Scripting.FileSystemObject")
        set d=fs.GetDrive("c:")
        Response.Write("The root folder is: " & d.RootFolder)
        set d=nothing
        set fs=nothing
%>
```
Output: The root folder is: C:\

8. The **SerialNumber** Property
The SerialNumber property returns the serial number of a specified drive.

Syntax - DriveObject.SerialNumber
Example
```
<%
    dim fs,d
    set fs=Server.CreateObject("Scripting.FileSystemObject")
    set d=fs.GetDrive("c:")
    Response.Write("The serial number is: " & d.SerialNumber)
    set d=nothing
    set fs=nothing
%>
```
Output: The serial number is: 474680516

8. The **ShareName** Property

The ShareName property returns the network share name for a specified drive.

Syntax - DriveObject.ShareName
Example
```
<%
    dim fs,d
    set fs=Server.CreateObject("Scripting.FileSystemObject")
    set d=fs.GetDrive("c:")
    Response.Write("The sharename is: " & d.ShareName)
    set d=nothing
    set fs=nothing
%>
```

9. The **TotalSize** Property

The TotalSize property returns the total size, in bytes, of a specified drive or network share.

Syntax - DriveObject.TotalSize

Example
```
<%
    dim fs,d
    set fs=Server.CreateObject("Scripting.FileSystemObject")
    set d=fs.GetDrive("c:")
    Response.Write("The total size in bytes is: " & d.TotalSize)
    set d=nothing
    set fs=nothing
%>
```
Output: The total size in bytes is: 4293563392

10. The **VolumeName** Property

The VolumeName property sets or returns the volume name of a specified drive.

Syntax - DriveObject.VolumeName[=newname]

Parameter	Description
newname	Optional. Sets the new name of the specified drive

Example

```
<%
    dim fs,d
    set fs=Server.CreateObject("Scripting.FileSystemObject")
    set d=fs.GetDrive("c:")
    Response.Write("The volume name is: " & d.VolumeName)
    set d=nothing
    set fs=nothing
%>
```

ASP File Object

The File object is used to return information about a specified file.

Examples

1. When was the file created?

```
<html> <body>
<%
dim fs, f
set fs=Server.CreateObject("Scripting.FileSystemObject")
set f=fs.GetFile(Server.MapPath("testread.txt"))
Response.Write("The file testread.txt was created on: " & f.DateCreated)
set f=nothing
set fs=nothing
%>
</body> </html>
```

2. When was the file last modified?

```
<html> <body>
<%
dim fs, f
set fs=Server.CreateObject("Scripting.FileSystemObject")
set f=fs.GetFile(Server.MapPath("testread.txt"))
Response.Write("The file testread.txt was last modified on: " &
f.DateLastModified)
set f=nothing
set fs=nothing
%>
</body> </html>
```

3. When was the file last accessed?

```
<html> <body>
<%
dim fs, f
set fs=Server.CreateObject("Scripting.FileSystemObject")
set f=fs.GetFile(Server.MapPath("testread.txt"))
Response.Write("The file testread.txt was last accessed on: " &
f.DateLastAccessed)
set f=nothing
set fs=nothing
%>
</body> </html>
```

4. Return the attributes of a specified file

```
<html> <body>
<%
set fs=Server.CreateObject("Scripting.FileSystemObject")
set f=fs.GetFile(Server.MapPath("testread.txt"))
Response.Write("The attributes of the file testread.txt are: " & f.Attributes)
set f=nothing      set fs=nothing %> </body> </html>
```

The File Object

The File object is used to return information about a specified file.

To work with the properties and methods of the File object, you will have to create an instance of the File object through the FileSystemObject object. First; create a FileSystemObject object and then instantiate the File object through the GetFile method of the FileSystemObject object or through the Files property of the Folder object.

The following code uses the GetFile method of the FileSystemObject object to instantiate the File object and the DateCreated property to return the date when the specified file was created:

```
<%
    Dim fs,f
    Set fs=Server.CreateObject("Scripting.FileSystemObject")
    Set f=fs.GetFile("c:\test.txt")
    Response.Write("File created: " & f.DateCreated)
    set f=nothing
    set fs=nothing
%>
```
Output: File created: 9/19/2001 10:01:19 AM

The File object's properties and methods are described below:

Properties

1. The **Attributes** Property

The Attributes property is used to set or return the attribute or attributes of a specified file or folder.

Syntax
```
    FileObject.Attributes[=newattributes]
    FolderObject.Attributes[=newattributes]
```

Parameter   Description

newattributes   Optional. Specifies the attribute value for the file or folder. Can take any of the following values or a combination of the following values:
0 = Normal file   1 = Read-only file   2 = Hidden file   4 = System file
16 = Folder or directory   32 = File has changed since last backup
1024 = Link or shortcut   2048 = Compressed file

Example for the File object
```
<%
    dim fs,f
    set fs=Server.CreateObject("Scripting.FileSystemObject")
    set f=fs.GetFile("c:\test.txt")
    Response.Write("The attributes of the file are: ")
    Response.Write(f.Attributes)
    set f=nothing
    set fs=nothing
%>
```
Output: The attributes of the file are: 32

Example for the Folder object

```
<%
      dim fs,fo
      set fs=Server.CreateObject("Scripting.FileSystemObject")
      set fo=fs.GetFolder("c:\test")
      Response.Write("The attributes of the folder are: ")
      Response.Write(fo.Attributes)
      set fo=nothing
      set fs=nothing
%>
```
Output: The attributes of the folder are: 16

2. The **DateCreated** Property
The DateCreated property is used to return the date and time when a specified file or folder was created.
Syntax –
FileObject.DateCreated
FolderObject.DateCreated

Example
```
<%
      dim fs,f
      set fs=Server.CreateObject("Scripting.FileSystemObject")
      set f=fs.GetFile("c:\test.txt")
      Response.Write("File created: ")
      Response.Write(f.DateCreated)
      // for folder
      set fo=fs.GetFolder("c:\test")
      Response.Write("Folder created: ")
      Response.Write(fo.DateCreated)
      set fo=nothing
      set f=nothing
      set fs=nothing
%>
```
Output: File created: 9/19/2001 10:01:19 AM
            Folder created: 9/19/2001 10:01:19 AM

3. The **DateLastAccessed** Property
The DateLastAccessed property is used to return the date and time when a specified file or folder was last accessed.

Syntax
      FileObject.DateLastAccessed
      FolderObject.DateLastAccessed

Example
```
<%
      dim fs,f
      set fs=Server.CreateObject("Scripting.FileSystemObject")
      set f=fs.GetFile("c:\test.txt")
      Response.Write("File last accessed on: ")
```

```
        Response.Write(f.DateLastAccessed)
        set fo=fs.GetFolder("c:\test")
        Response.Write("Folder last accessed on: ")
        Response.Write(fo.DateLastAccessed)
        set fo=nothing
        set f=nothing
        set fs=nothing
%>
```
Output: File last accessed on: 10/29/2001 10:21:23 AM
        Folder last accessed on: 9/19/2001 10:01:19 AM

4. The **DateLastModified** Property

The DateLastModified property is used to return the date and time when a specified file or folder was last modified.

Syntax

        FileObject.DateLastModified
        FolderObject.DateLastModified

Example
```
<%
        dim fs,f
        set fs=Server.CreateObject("Scripting.FileSystemObject")
        set f=fs.GetFile("c:\test.txt")
        Response.Write("File last modified on: ")
        Response.Write(f.DateLastModified)
        set fo=fs.GetFolder("c:\test")
        Response.Write("Folder last modified on: ")
        Response.Write(fo.DateLastModified)
        set fo=nothing
        set f=nothing
        set fs=nothing
%>
```
Output: File last modified on: 1/10/2001 10:01:19 AM
        Folder last modified on: 9/19/2001 10:01:19 AM

5. The **Drive** Property

The Drive property is used to return the drive letter of the drive where the specified file or folder resides.

Syntax

        FileObject.Drive
        FolderObject.Drive

Example
```
<%
    dim fs,f
    set fs=Server.CreateObject("Scripting.FileSystemObject")
    set f=fs.GetFile("c:\test.txt")
    Response.Write("File resides on drive: ")
    Response.Write(f.Drive)
    set f=nothing
    set fs=nothing
%>
```
Output: File resides on drive: c:

5. The **Name** Property
The Name property is used to set or return the name of a specified file or folder.

Syntax
```
FileObject.Name[=newname]
FolderObject.Name[=newname]
```

Parameter	Description
newname	Optional. Specifies the name of the file or folder

Example
```
<%
    dim fs,f
    set fs=Server.CreateObject("Scripting.FileSystemObject")
    set f=fs.GetFile("c:\test.txt")
    Response.Write("The file's name: ")
    Response.Write(f.Name)
    set fo=fs.GetFolder("c:\test")
    Response.Write("The folder's name: ")
    Response.Write(fo.Name)
    set fo=nothing
    set f=nothing
    set fs=nothing
%>
```
Output: The file's name: test.txt
        The folder's name: test

7. The **ParentFolder** Property
The ParentFolder property is used to return the folder object for the parent of the specified file or folder.

Syntax
```
FileObject.ParentFolder
FolderObject.ParentFolder
```

Example
```
<%
        dim fs,f
        set fs=Server.CreateObject("Scripting.FileSystemObject")
        set f=fs.GetFile("c:\asp\test\test.asp")
        Response.Write("The file test.asp is in the folder: ")
        Response.Write(f.ParentFolder)
        set fo=fs.GetFolder("c:\asp\test")
        Response.Write("The folder test is in the folder: ")
        Response.Write(fo.ParentFolder)
        set fo=nothing
        set f=nothing
        set fs=nothing
%>
```
Output: The file test.asp is in the folder: C:\asp\test
        The folder test is in the folder: C:\asp

8. The **ParentFolder** Property
The ParentFolder property is used to return the folder object for the parent of the specified file or folder.
Syntax
        FileObject.ParentFolder
        FolderObject.ParentFolder

Example
```
<%
        dim fs,f
        set fs=Server.CreateObject("Scripting.FileSystemObject")
        set f=fs.GetFile("c:\asp\test\test.asp")
        Response.Write("The file test.asp is in the folder: ")
        Response.Write(f.ParentFolder)
        set fo=fs.GetFolder("c:\asp\test")
        Response.Write("The folder test is in the folder: ")
        Response.Write(fo.ParentFolder)
        set fo=nothing
        set f=nothing
        set fs=nothing
%>
```
Output: The file test.asp is in the folder: C:\asp\test
        The folder test is in the folder: C:\asp

10. The **ShortName** Property
The ShortName property is used to return the short name of a specified file or folder (the 8.3 naming convention).

Syntax
        FileObject.ShortName
        FolderObject.ShortName

Example
```
<%
      dim fs,f
      set fs=Server.CreateObject("Scripting.FileSystemObject")
      set f=fs.GetFile("c:\hitcounterfile.txt"))
      Response.Write("Name: " & f.Name)
      Response.Write("<br />ShortName: " & f.ShortName)
      set fo=fs.GetFolder("c:\asp_test_web")
      Response.Write("Name: " & fo.Name)
      Response.Write("<br />ShortName: " & fo.ShortName)
      set fo=nothing
      set f=nothing
      set fs=nothing
%>
```
Output:
Name: hitcounterfile.txt
ShortName: HITCOU~1.TXT
Name: asp_test_web
ShortName: ASP_TE~1

11. The **ShortPath** Property
The ShortPath property is used to return the short path of the specified file or folder (the 8.3 naming convention).

Syntax
      FileObject.ShortPath
      FolderObject.ShortPath

Example
```
<%
      dim fs,f
      set fs=Server.CreateObject("Scripting.FileSystemObject")
      set f=fs.GetFile("c:\asp_test_web\hitcounterfile.txt")
      Response.Write("Path: " & f.Path)
      Response.Write("<br />ShortPath: " & f.ShortPath)
      set fo=fs.GetFolder("c:\asp_test_web")
      Response.Write("Path: " & fo.Path)
      Response.Write("<br />ShortPath: " & fo.ShortPath)
      set fo=nothing
      set f=nothing
      set fs=nothing
%>
```
Output:
      Path: C:\asp_test_web\hitcounterfile.txt
      ShortPath: C:\ASP_TE~1\HITCOU~1.TXT
      Path: C:\asp_test_web
      ShortPath: C:\ASP_TE~1

12. The **Size** Property

The Size property is used to return the size, in bytes, of the specified file or folder.

Syntax
        FileObject.Size
        FolderObject.Size

Example
```
<%
        dim fs,f
        set fs=Server.CreateObject("Scripting.FileSystemObject")
        set f=fs.GetFile("c:\test.asp")
        Response.Write("The size of test.asp is: ")
        Response.Write(f.Size & " bytes.")
        set fo=fs.GetFolder("c:\test")
        Response.Write("The size of the folder test is: ")
        Response.Write(fo.Size & " bytes.")
        set fo=nothing
        set f=nothing
        set fs=nothing
%>
```
Output:
The size of test.asp is: 10556 bytes.
The size of the folder test is: 123456 bytes.

13. The **Type** Property

The Type property is used to return the type of the specified file or folder.

Syntax
        FileObject.Type
        FolderObject.Type

Examples
```
<%
        dim fs,f
        set fs=Server.CreateObject("Scripting.FileSystemObject")
        set f=fs.GetFile("c:test.txt")
        Response.Write("The file test.txt is of type: ")
        Response.Write(f.Type)
        set f=nothing
        set fs=nothing
%>
```
Output: The file test.txt is of type: Text Document

Methods

1. The **Copy** Method

The Copy method copies the specified file or folder from one location to another.

Syntax
> FileObject.Copy(destination[,overwrite])
> FolderObject.Copy(destination[,overwrite])

Parameter	Description
destination	Required. Where to copy the file or folder. Wildcard characters are not allowed

overwrite   Optional. A Boolean value indicating whether an existing file or folder can be overwritten. True indicates that the file/folder can be overwritten, false indicates that the file/folder cannot be overwritten. Default is true.

Example for the File object
```
<%
    dim fs,f
    set fs=Server.CreateObject("Scripting.FileSystemObject")
    set f=fs.GetFile("c:\test.txt")
    f.Copy("c:\new_test.txt",false)
    set fo=fs.GetFolder("c:\test")
    fo.Copy("c:\new_test",false)
    set fo=nothing
    set f=nothing
    set fs=nothing
%>
```

2. The **Delete** Method

The Delete method deletes a specified file or folder.

Syntax
> FileObject.Delete[(force)]
> FolderObject.Delete[(force)]

Parameter	Description
force	Optional. A Boolean value that indicates whether a read-only file or folder are to be deleted. True indicates that a read-only file/folder will be deleted and false indicates that it will not be deleted. Default is false.

Example
```
<%
    dim fs,f
    set fs=Server.CreateObject("Scripting.FileSystemObject")
    set f=fs.GetFile("c:\test.txt")
```

```
        f.Delete
        set fo=fs.GetFolder("c:\test")
        fo.Delete
        set fo=nothing
        set f=nothing
set fs=nothing %>
```
3. The **Move** Method
The Move method moves the specified file or folder from one location to another.

Syntax
```
        FileObject.Move(destination)
        FolderObject.Move(destination)
```

Parameter	Description
destination	Required. Where to move the file or folder. Wildcard characters are not allowed

Example
```
<%
dim fs,f
set fs=Server.CreateObject("Scripting.FileSystemObject")
Set f=fs.GetFile("c:\test.txt")
f.Move("c:\test\")
set f=nothing
set fs=nothing
%>
```

4. The **OpenAsTextStream** Method
The OpenAsTextStream method opens the specified file and returns a TextStream object to access the file.
Syntax - FileObject.OpenAsTextStream(mode,format)

Parameter	Description
mode	Optional. How to open the file. 1 = ForReading - Open a file for reading. You cannot write to this file 2 = ForWriting - Open a file for writing 8 = ForAppending - Open a file and write to the end of the file
format	Optional. The format of the file. 0 = TristateFalse - Default. Open the file as ASCII -1 = TristateTrue - Open the file as Unicode -2 = TristateUseDefault - Open the file using the system default

Example
```
<%
        dim fs,f,ts
        set fs=Server.CreateObject("Scripting.FileSystemObject")
```

```
        Set f=fs.GetFile("c:\test.txt")
        Set ts=f.OpenAsTextStream(ForWriting)
        ts.Write("Hello World!")
        ts.Close
        Set ts=f.OpenAsTextStream(ForReading)
        Response.Write(ts.ReadAll)
        ts.Close
        set ts=nothing
        set f=nothing
        set fs=nothing
%>
Output: Hello World!
```

ASP Folder Object

The Folder object is used to return information about a specified folder. To work with the properties and methods of the Folder object, you will have to create an instance of the Folder object through the FileSystemObject object. First; create a FileSystemObject object and then instantiate the Folder object through the GetFolder method of the FileSystemObject object.

The following code uses the GetFolder method of the FileSystemObject object to instantiate the Folder object and the DateCreated property to return the date when the specified folder was created:

```
<%
        Dim fs,fo
        Set fs=Server.CreateObject("Scripting.FileSystemObject")
        Set fo=fs.GetFolder("c:\test")
        Response.Write("Folder created: " & fo.DateCreated)
        set fo=nothing
        set fs=nothing
%>
Output: Folder created: 10/22/2001 10:01:19 AM
```

The Folder object's collections, properties, and methods are described below:

Collections
1. The **Files** Collection
The Files collection returns a collection of all the files in a specified folder.
Syntax - FolderObject.Files

Example
```
<%
        dim fs,fo,x
        set fs=Server.CreateObject("Scripting.FileSystemObject")
        set fo=fs.GetFolder("c:\test\")
        for each x in fo.files
          'Print the name of all files in the test folder
          Response.write(x.Name & "<br />")
        next
%>
```

Output:
test_adv.txt
guestbook.txt
links.txt
links2.txt
textads.txt
textfile.txt

2. The **SubFolders** Collection

The SubFolders collection returns a collection of all subfolders in a specified folder.

Syntax- FolderObject.SubFolders

Example
```
<%
    dim fs,fo,x
    set fs=Server.CreateObject("Scripting.FileSystemObject")
    set fo=fs.GetFolder("c:\test\")
    for each x in fo.SubFolders
     'Print the name of all subfolders in the test folder
     Response.write(x.Name & "<br />")
    next
    set fo=nothing
    set fs=nothing
%>
```
Output:
html
css
asp

Properties

Property	Description
Attributes	Sets or returns the attributes of a specified folder
DateCreated	Returns the date and time when a specified folder was created
DateLastAccessed	Returns the date and time when a specified folder was last accessed
DateLastModified	Returns the date and time when a specified folder was last modified
Drive	Returns the drive letter of the drive where the specified folder resides
IsRootFolder	Returns true if a folder is the root folder and false if not
Name	Sets or returns the name of a specified folder
ParentFolder	Returns the parent folder of a specified folder
Path	Returns the path for a specified folder
ShortName	Returns the short name of a specified folder
ShortPath	Returns the short path of a specified folder
Size	Returns the size of a specified folder
Type	Returns the type of a specified folder

ASP TextStream Object

The TextStream object is used to access the contents of a text file.

Examples - Read textfile

```
<html> <body>
<p>This is the text in the text file:</p>
<%
Set fs=Server.CreateObject("Scripting.FileSystemObject")

Set f=fs.OpenTextFile(Server.MapPath("testread.txt"), 1)
Response.Write(f.ReadAll)
f.Close

Set f=Nothing
Set fs=Nothing
%>
</body> </html>
```

This example demonstrates how to use the OpenTextFile method of the FileSystemObject to create a TextStream Object. The ReadAll method of the TextStream Object reads from the opened text file.

Read only a part of a textfile

```
<html> <body>
<p>This is the first five characters from the text file:</p>
<%
Set fs=Server.CreateObject("Scripting.FileSystemObject")

Set f=fs.OpenTextFile(Server.MapPath("testread.txt"), 1)
Response.Write(f.Read(5))
f.Close
%>
</body> </html>
```

Read one line of a textfile

```
<html><body>
<p>This is the first line of the text file:</p>
<%
Set fs=Server.CreateObject("Scripting.FileSystemObject")
Set f=fs.OpenTextFile(Server.MapPath("testread.txt"), 1)
Response.Write(f.ReadLine)
f.Close
Set f=Nothing
Set fs=Nothing
%>
</body> </html>
```

Read all lines from a textfile

```
<html> <body>
<p>This is all the lines in the text file:</p>

<%
Set fs=Server.CreateObject("Scripting.FileSystemObject")
Set f=fs.OpenTextFile(Server.MapPath("testread.txt"), 1)

do while f.AtEndOfStream = false
Response.Write(f.ReadLine)
Response.Write("<br>")
loop

f.Close
Set f=Nothing
Set fs=Nothing
%>
</body> </html>
```

Skip a part of a textfile

```
<html> <body>
<p>The first four characters in the text file are skipped:</p>
<%
Set fs=Server.CreateObject("Scripting.FileSystemObject")
Set f=fs.OpenTextFile(Server.MapPath("testread.txt"), 1)
f.Skip(4)
Response.Write(f.ReadAll)
f.Close
Set f=Nothing
Set fs=Nothing
%> </body> </html>
```

Skip a line of a textfile

```
<html> <body>
<p>The first line in the text file is skipped:</p>
<%
Set fs=Server.CreateObject("Scripting.FileSystemObject")
Set f=fs.OpenTextFile(Server.MapPath("testread.txt"), 1)
f.SkipLine
Response.Write(f.ReadAll)
f.Close
Set f=Nothing
Set fs=Nothing
%>
</body> </html>
```

Return line-number

```
<html> <body>
<p>This is all the lines in the text file (with line numbers):</p>
<% Set fs=Server.CreateObject("Scripting.FileSystemObject")
```

```
Set f=fs.OpenTextFile(Server.MapPath("testread.txt"), 1)
do while f.AtEndOfStream = false
Response.Write("Line:" & f.Line & " ")
Response.Write(f.ReadLine)
Response.Write("<br>")
loop
f.Close
Set f=Nothing
Set fs=Nothing
%> </body> </html>
```

Get column number
```
<html> <body>
<%
Set fs=Server.CreateObject("Scripting.FileSystemObject")
Set f=fs.OpenTextFile(Server.MapPath("testread.txt"), 1)
Response.Write(f.Read(2))
Response.Write("<p>The cursor is now standing in position " & f.Column & "
in the text file.</p>")
f.Close
Set f=Nothing
Set fs=Nothing
%> </body> </html>,
```

The TextStream Object
The TextStream object is used to access the contents of text files.
The following code creates a text file (c:\test.txt) and then writes some text to
the file (the variable f is an instance of the TextStream object):
```
<%
dim fs, f
set fs=Server.CreateObject("Scripting.FileSystemObject")
set f=fs.CreateTextFile("c:\test.txt",true)
f.WriteLine("Hello World!")
f.Close
set f=nothing
set fs=nothing
%>
```

To create an instance of the TextStream object you can use the
CreateTextFile or OpenTextFile methods of the FileSystemObject object, or
you can use the OpenAsTextStream method of the File object.

The TextStream object's properties and methods are described below:
Properties

Property	Description
AtEndOfLine	Returns true if the file pointer is positioned immediately before the end-of-line marker in a TextStream file, and false if not
AtEndOfStream	Returns true if the file pointer is at the end of a TextStream file, and false if not

Column	Returns the column number of the current character position in an input stream
Line	Returns the current line number in a TextStream file

1. The AtEndOfLine Property

The AtEndOfLine property returns a Boolean value. True indicates that the file pointer is positioned immediately before the end-of-line marker in a TextStream file. Otherwise, it returns False.

Note: This property will only work on a TextStream object that are open for reading.

Syntax - TextStreamObject.AtEndOfLine

Example

```
<%
dim fs,f,t,x
set fs=Server.CreateObject("Scripting.FileSystemObject")
set f=fs.CreateTextFile("c:\test.txt")
f.write("Hello World!")
f.close
set t=fs.OpenTextFile("c:\test.txt",1,false)
do while t.AtEndOfLine<>true
  x=t.Read(1)
loop
t.close
Response.Write("The last character is: " & x)
%>
Output:  The last character of the first line in the text file is: !
```

2. The **AtEndOfStream** Property

The AtEndOfStream property returns True if the file pointer is at the end of a TextStream file, and False if not.

Note: This property will only work on a TextStream object that are open for reading.

Syntax - TextStreamObject.AtEndOfStream

Example

```
<%
dim fs,f,t,x
set fs=Server.CreateObject("Scripting.FileSystemObject")
set f=fs.CreateTextFile("c:\test.txt")
f.write("Hello World!")
f.close
set t=fs.OpenTextFile("c:\test.txt",1,false)
do while t.AtEndOfStream<>true
  x=t.Read(1)
loop
t.close
Response.Write("The last character is: " & x)
```

```
%>
```
Output: The last character in the text file is: !

3. The **Column** Property

The Column property returns the column number of the current character position in an input stream.

Note: This property is 1 after a new line character is written (even before any other character is written).

Syntax - TextStreamObject.Column

```
<%
dim fs,f,t,x,y
set fs=Server.CreateObject("Scripting.FileSystemObject")
set f=fs.CreateTextFile("c:\test.txt")
f.write("Hello World!")
f.close
set t=fs.OpenTextFile("c:\test.txt",1,false)
do while t.AtEndOfStream<>true
  x=t.Read(1)
  y=t.Column-1
loop
t.close
Response.Write("The last character in the text file is: " & x)
Response.Write("<br /> at character position: " & y)
%>
```
Output:
The last character in the text file is: !
at character position: 12

4. The **Line** Property

The Line property returns the current line number in a TextStream file (starting at 1).

Syntax - TextStreamObject.Line

Example

```
<%
dim fs,f,t
set fs=Server.CreateObject("Scripting.FileSystemObject")
set f=fs.CreateTextFile("c:\test.txt",true)
f.WriteLine("Hello World!")
f.WriteLine("How are you today?")
f.WriteLine("Goodbye!")
f.close
Set t=fs.OpenTextFile("c:\test.txt",1)
do while t.AtEndOfStream=false
  Response.Write("Line " & t.Line & ": ")
  Response.Write(t.ReadLine)
  Response.Write("<br>")
loop
t.Close
```

```
%>
```

Output:
Line 1: Hello World!
Line 2: Hoe are you today?
Line 3: Goodbye!

Methods
1. The **Close** Method
The Close method closes an open TextStream file.
Syntax - TextStreamObject.Close

Example
```
<%
dim fs,f
set fs=Server.CreateObject("Scripting.FileSystemObject")
set f=fs.CreateTextFile("c:\test.txt",true)
f.WriteLine("Hello World!")
f.Close
set f=nothing
set fs=nothing
%>
```

2. The **Read** Method
The Read method reads a specified number of characters from a TextStream file and returns the result as a string.
Syntax - TextStreamObject.Read(numchar)

Parameter	Description
numchar	Required. The number of characters to read from the file

Example
```
<%
dim fs,f,t,x
set fs=Server.CreateObject("Scripting.FileSystemObject")
set f=fs.CreateTextFile("c:\test.txt")
f.write("Hello World!")
f.close
set t=fs.OpenTextFile("c:\test.txt",1,false)
x=t.Read(5)
t.close
Response.Write("The first five characters are: " & x)
%>
Output: The first five characters are: Hello
```

3. The **ReadAll** Method
The ReadAll method reads an entire TextStream file and returns the result as a string.
Note: This method is not suitable for large files (it wastes memory resources).

Syntax - TextStreamObject.ReadAll

Example
```
<%
dim fs,f,t,x
set fs=Server.CreateObject("Scripting.FileSystemObject")
set f=fs.CreateTextFile("c:\test.txt")
f.write("Hello World!")
f.close
set t=fs.OpenTextFile("c:\test.txt",1,false)
x=t.ReadAll
t.close
Response.Write("The text in the file is: " & x)
%>
Output: The text in the file is: Hello World!
```

4. The **ReadLine** Method
The ReadLine method reads one line from a TextStream file and returns the result as a string.

Syntax - TextStreamObject.ReadLine
Example
```
<%
dim fs,f,t,x
set fs=Server.CreateObject("Scripting.FileSystemObject")
set f=fs.CreateTextFile("c:\test.txt")
f.writeline("Line 1")
f.writeline("Line 2")
f.writeline("Line 3")
f.close
set t=fs.OpenTextFile("c:\test.txt",1,false)
x=t.ReadLine
t.close
Response.Write("The first line in the file ")
Response.Write("contains this text: " & x)
%>
Output: The first line in the file contains this text: Line 1
```

5. The **Skip** Method
The Skip method skips a specified number of characters when reading a TextStream file.
Syntax - TextStreamObject.Skip(numchar)

Parameter	Description
numchar	Required. The number of characters to skip

Example
```
<%
dim fs,f,t,x
set fs=Server.CreateObject("Scripting.FileSystemObject")
```

```
set f=fs.CreateTextFile("c:\test.txt")
f.write("Hello World!")
f.close
set t=fs.OpenTextFile("c:\test.txt",1,false)
t.Skip(7)
x=t.ReadAll
t.close
Response.Write("The output after skipping some characters: " & x)
%>
Output: The output after skipping some characters: orld!
```

6. The **SkipLine** Method

The SkipLine method skips a line when reading a TextStream file.

Syntax - TextStreamObject.SkipLine
Example

```
<%
dim fs,f,t,x
set fs=Server.CreateObject("Scripting.FileSystemObject")
set f=fs.CreateTextFile("c:\test.txt")
f.writeline("Line 1")
f.writeline("Line 2")
f.writeline("Line 3")
f.close
set t=fs.OpenTextFile("c:\test.txt",1,false)
t.SkipLine
x=t.ReadAll
t.close
Response.Write("Output after skipping the first ")
Response.Write(" line in the file: " & x)
%>
Output: Output after skipping the first line in the file: Line 2
Line 3
```

7. The **Write** Method

The Write method writes a specified text to a TextStream file.
Note: This method write text to the TextStream file with no spaces or line breaks between each string.
Syntax - TextStreamObject.Write(text)

Parameter	Description
text	Required. The text to write to the file

Example

```
<%
dim fs,f
set fs=Server.CreateObject("Scripting.FileSystemObject")
set f=fs.CreateTextFile("c:\test.txt",true)
f.write("Hello World!")
f.write("How are you today?")
```

```
f.close
set f=nothing
set fs=nothing
%>
```
The file test.txt will look like this after executing the code above:
Hello World!How are you today?

8. The **WriteLine** Method
The WriteLine method writes a specified text and a new-line character to a TextStream file.

Syntax - TextStreamObject.WriteLine(text)

Example
```
<%
dim fs,f
set fs=Server.CreateObject("Scripting.FileSystemObject")
set f=fs.CreateTextFile("c:\test.txt",true)
f.WriteLine("Hello World!")
f.WriteLine("How are you today?")
f.WriteLine("Goodbye!")
f.close
set f=nothing
set fs=nothing
%>
```
The file test.txt will look like this after executing the code above:
Hello World!
How are you today?
Goodbye!

9. The **WriteBlankLines** Method
The WriteBlankLines method writes a specified number of new-line characters to a TextStream file.
Syntax - TextStreamObject.WriteBlankLines(numlines)

Example
```
<%
dim fs,f
set fs=Server.CreateObject("Scripting.FileSystemObject")
set f=fs.CreateTextFile("c:\test.txt",true)
f.WriteLine("Hello World!")
f.WriteBlankLines(2)
f.WriteLine("How are you today?")
f.close
set f=nothing
set fs=nothing
%>
```
The file test.txt will look like this after executing the code above:
Hello World!
How are you today?

ASP Drive Object
The Drive object is used to return information about a local disk drive or a network share.

Examples
Get the available space of a specified drive
```
<html> <body>
<% Dim fs, d, n
Set fs=Server.CreateObject("Scripting.FileSystemObject")
Set d=fs.GetDrive("c:")
n = "Drive: " & d
n = n & "<br>Available Space in bytes: " & d.AvailableSpace
Response.Write(n)
set d=nothing
set fs=nothing
%> </body> </html>
```

Get the free space of a specified drive
```
<html> <body>
<%
Dim fs, d, n
Set fs=Server.CreateObject("Scripting.FileSystemObject")
Set d=fs.GetDrive("c:")
n = "Drive: " & d
n = n & "<br />Free Space in bytes: " & d.FreeSpace
Response.Write(n)
set d=nothing
set fs=nothing
%> </body> </html>
```

Get the total size of a specified drive
```
<html> <body>
<%
Dim fs,d,n
Set fs=Server.CreateObject("Scripting.FileSystemObject")
Set d=fs.GetDrive("c:")
n = "Drive: " & d
n = n & "<br>Total size in bytes: " & d.TotalSize
Response.Write(n)
set d=nothing
set fs=nothing
%> </body> </html>
```
Get the drive letter of a specified drive
```
<html> <body>
<%
dim fs, d, n
set fs=Server.CreateObject("Scripting.FileSystemObject")
set d=fs.GetDrive("c:")
Response.Write("The drive letter is: " & d.driveletter)
set d=nothing
```

```
set fs=nothing
%>
</body> </html>
```

Get the drive type of a specified drive
```
<html> <body>
<%
dim fs, d, n
set fs=Server.CreateObject("Scripting.FileSystemObject")
set d=fs.GetDrive("c:")
Response.Write("The drive type is: " & d.DriveType)
set d=nothing
set fs=nothing
%> </body> </html>
```

Get the file system of a specified drive
```
<html> <body>
<%
dim fs, d, n
set fs=Server.CreateObject("Scripting.FileSystemObject")
set d=fs.GetDrive("c:")
Response.Write("The file system is: " & d.FileSystem)
set d=nothing
set fs=nothing
%> </body> </html>
```

Is the drive ready?
```
<html> <body>
<%
dim fs,d,n
set fs=Server.CreateObject("Scripting.FileSystemObject")
set d=fs.GetDrive("c:")
n = "The " & d.DriveLetter
if d.IsReady=true then
    n = n & " drive is ready."
else
    n = n & " drive is not ready."
end if
Response.Write(n)
set d=nothing
set fs=nothing
%> </body> </html>
```

Get the path of a specified drive
```
<html> <body>
<%
dim fs,d
set fs=Server.CreateObject("Scripting.FileSystemObject")
set d=fs.GetDrive("c:")
```

```
Response.Write("The path is " & d.Path)
set d=nothing
set fs=nothing
%></body> </html>
```

Get the root folder of a specified drive
```
<html> <body>
<%
dim fs,d
set fs=Server.CreateObject("Scripting.FileSystemObject")
set d=fs.GetDrive("c:")
Response.Write("The rootfolder is " & d.RootFolder)
set d=nothing
set fs=nothing
%> </body> </html>
```

Get the serialnumber of a specified drive
```
<html> <body>
<%
dim fs,d
set fs=Server.CreateObject("Scripting.FileSystemObject")
set d=fs.GetDrive("c:")
Response.Write("The serialnumber is " & d.SerialNumber)
set d=nothing
set fs=nothing
%> </body> </html>
```